Can You See Me Yet?

There Is More to Learn

Using Understanding to Help Students
of Poverty Feel Seen, Understood &
Valued in the Classroom

Can You See Me Yet?

There Is More to Learn

Using Understanding to Help Students of
Poverty Feel Seen, Understood &
Valued in the Classroom

Belinda Adams

Certified Childhood Trauma Professional

Anchor Book Press · Palatine

Can You See Me Yet? There Is More to Learn: Using Understanding to Help Students of Poverty Feel Seen, Understood, and Valued in the Classroom.

Copyright © 2020 Belinda Adams
Published by Anchor Book Press, Ltd
440 W Colfax Road, Palatine, IL 60078
ISBN: 9781949109511
Library of Congress Control Number: 2020942522
Printed in the United States

Dedication

This book is dedicated to my editor, publisher and dear friend, Carol Pirog of Anchor Book Press, Ltd. We met each other as teachers and became inseparable friends due to our passion for our students and love for our jobs. She's read my anxious texts at midnight because I couldn't wait until morning to hear what she thought of the latest manuscript, and answered phone calls while on vacation and at the doctor's office.

Thank you, Carol, for everything you do!

Acknowledgements

I'm probably going to shock a few educators here when I acknowledge some of my previous administrators. They will know who they are after reading this book. They were the administrators who recognized, first and foremost, my passion for teaching and my love for my students. Secondly, they noticed I was a pretty savvy educator, and if left to my own devices in the classroom, my students would show some awesome academic and emotional growth. Thank you, for having confidence in my abilities, for supporting me when I struggled, and for allowing me to be the best educator I could be!

Knowing the traumatic realities of poverty (or understanding these disparities might be part of a student's life) might be the only way you can help a child overcome the sadness and hopelessness that poverty brings.

~Belinda Adams, Educator, Author

Foreword

To the reader I would like to say, Belinda Adams' first book, *Can You See Me?* presents some radical, yet simple concepts. *Can You See Me Yet? There Is More to Learn,* is built on that foundation. You will find if you think about it, these concepts and strategies make complete sense. The ideas presented here are strategies you can begin to incorporate in your classroom tomorrow, but it will take a lifetime tweaking them to fit your teaching style and your students' needs. With stories that cause us to laugh and to cry, Belinda reminds us that one size does not fit all. If we want to succeed and more importantly, if we want our students to succeed, it is essential that we look for and meet the needs of each student.

In *Can You See Me Yet? There Is More to Learn,* Belinda shares what works. She's also candid about her mistakes and shares the valuable lessons she learned from them that have benefitted her students. Belinda shows us that teaching is a humbling job; we may not always get it right but we have a chance to make things right if we're willing to make changes. It has worked for her and it can work for you.

When I first met Belinda, she'd agree that she was a bit naïve in believing all children want to learn. In a school with predominantly poor children, she learned that naiveté is often a target for students who aren't afraid to let their teacher know they see right through her. Her first years of teaching were a struggle and she often felt frustrated and incompetent at the end of the day. That's when Belinda began the quest to change herself – to become the teacher her students needed, not the one she envisioned herself to be. Because those two concepts were not compatible (especially when first attempting to change her habits and approaches).

Data has always been interesting to me. It wasn't necessarily about being competitive with other teachers; I just liked to examine the mid-year and year-end growth data for students. Belinda's student data demonstrated the highest level of growth. Working with the most difficult students, year after year, her numbers were on top. Students that had previously shown very little growth, were making 1, 2 and even 3 years academic growth. I once heard Belinda tell her students, "You're not going to fail. I won't let you. We're in this together."

Over the years, her excellent data didn't change, even with mandates from administration to use this program or that program. Because it is not the program, it's the people. Research has shown, the teacher is the most important variable that schools have in their arsenal. Belinda illustrates to educators and administrators that teachers who really care can make the biggest impression on their students, and ultimately, help students to show excellent academic growth as well.

Belinda is one of the most caring teachers I know. While all the rest of us were praying that we didn't get that difficult kid, Belinda saw each child as an opportunity for change. Not only that, and I believe this is another key to her success, she loves those difficult kids and she loves her job. She didn't stop there. She's spent the last ten years educating herself and other educators (through her books, workshops and on-the-job experiences) about how poverty and trauma impact children. She's developed a toolbox of approaches she can pull from to meet the needs of her individual students. She's tried many strategies since I've known her. She'll be honest and tell you that many have been successful and a few of them died a quick death. Some are skills, some are strategies, and some are just how to understand and connect with your students.

As a Certified Childhood Trauma Professional, Belinda takes the concepts she has learned and applies them daily in her classroom. Her efforts are not rocket science; however, they require a dedication to your students, a willingness to change, and a desire to connect with your students in a meaningful way that motivates them to learn.

Belinda wrote *Can You See Me Yet? There is More to Learn* because, she believes, there is always more to learn about ways to create a classroom environment that builds self-esteem, fosters emotional regulation, and encourages learning. The concepts in this book are essential to your success and your students; they don't cost a lot of money or a lot of time, just a willingness to do what it takes to make a difference.

~ Annie Moore – Educator and Author

Table of Contents

Introduction

It's been a few years since I wrote *Can You See Me?* It was my first book, and it was the culmination of stories I had filed away from the previous 15 years of teaching. I've had educators and others say, "Thank you for sharing your stories." I've always answered, "Thank my students. It was their stories I was telling; reliving their challenges and their successes, and our experiences together."

I can honestly say that even the most difficult students have taught me valuable lessons about how to challenge myself to think outside of the box – to look for strategies, solutions, and okay, tricks to get them to engage and learn. And I'd like to think that those times when I've had to step up to the plate under pressure I came out as a more compassionate educator. I also felt I was better prepared for the next challenging student who sat in my classroom.

In my previous books, I broadened the scope from poverty to trauma, an all-inclusive umbrella that included poverty. While many of the strategies that help students of trauma benefit all students, it always seems that, in my mind, children of poverty have another set of issues, and often, those issues require unique strategies that don't apply to all children of trauma.

If you asked one of my low-income students if he was poor, he would say, "No, I'm not." Because most of them don't see themselves living in poverty; unfortunately, that may be all they know. That "unknowing" or denial, whatever you'd like to call it, can create situations in the classroom where many teachers feel at a loss as to what to do. If you've read my previous books, you know that a great deal of my classroom strategies were "let's give this a try" ideas, because when you're dealing with students of poverty and trauma, there is no one fix for every child. Other strategies have taken entire summers to think through, revise, start over, and plan to implement for the fall. Still sadly, even some of these well thought-out ideas fail for many students, and it's necessary to go back to the drawing table.

The common theme throughout it all: never give up because every child deserves the best effort we have to offer. In fact, we (educators) may be all that stands between them and continued failure and generational poverty. This book is for those who want to be the difference between success and failure – between happiness and hopelessness. I've witnessed it; I've felt my heartstrings stretched to the point of tears when students have let down their guard and allowed themselves to be touched and moved to reach greater heights than they ever dreamed possible. Those successes, those moments of sheer exhilaration, are what drive me to continue to learn and to be the best teacher I can.

It really doesn't have to be about educators devoting 15 hours a week to planning or feeling frustrated every day. It's not one or the other. It's a long road to retirement if you decide it has to be one way or the other. Once you've implemented the key strategies that empower your students to succeed, it's an issue of showing up and being the best you can be each and every day. Your students will respond!

Belinda Adams

Poverty is Trauma

Research shows that 21% of American children live in poverty, meaning their families earns less than $25,500 per year. In many instances, the children that I have met live with income far below that. Yet, the students I've worked with would never tell you they were poor or "poverty stricken." Either due to pride or little knowledge of their circumstances. Students of poverty do not know that their life situations impact everything they do: their relationships with their peers, their interactions with adults, and most importantly, their education.

In addition to the changes in a child's brain (which I'll discuss later) due to the stress of trauma, such as poverty, these children experience developmental consequences as well, including:

- Difficulty trusting others
- Social isolation
- Difficulty seeking help
- Hypersensitivity to physical contact
- Increased medical, emotional and mental problems
- Poor affect regulation
- Problems with academic achievement
- Oppositional/antisocial behaviors
- Difficulty planning for the future (Ingram).

If you notice from the previous list, most of these factors will influence our students in the classroom. How we choose to deal with these developmental issues may determine the difference between a classroom that functions well where learning is a priority or a classroom with disorganized, disrespectful, and disengaged children.

In addition, we have to take into consideration that, "The poorest children showed the most delays in brain development and had the lowest academic achievement scores" (Rocheleau, 2019). While this information is helpful in understanding why some children of poverty fail to meet academic benchmarks compared to their middle-class peers, it takes strategies like those illustrated in this book to reverse the negative effects of poverty on the brain and positively impact their future academic achievement and emotional regulation.

Article author Rocheleau states that some of the negative impact on the brain can be reversed through "education and positive interactions with parents" (2019). Teachers have little control in how children interact with their parents, and as I've written in all of my books, it's impossible to control or even know all of the interactions our students face when they leave us each day. We've got to rely on the strategies we can incorporate at school, such as building rapport, developing a school/home connection, and focusing on appropriate instructional techniques that support our students in a way that encourages them to want to learn.

Students of poverty are not unlike other children. Deep inside, they long for acceptance and success. They disguise these needs with behaviors, such as indifference, low motivation, frustration and sheer inflexibility. They expect teachers to give up; to throw their hands up in frustration and walk way.

If you're dedicated to your profession, and just stubborn like me, these children represent crying hearts reaching out for understanding and love. Poverty is trauma, and if we want these students to be successful, we have to treat poverty as trauma.

Belinda Adams

Chapter 1

Reigning In Unpredictable Emotions

Belinda Adams

The Brain of the Poverty Student

It has been well researched and documented that children of trauma, poverty included, have differences in their brain development when compared to their same-age peers who have not experienced a traumatic event. Studies have concluded that children who experience continued stress – such as that experienced by children living in poverty – can develop an atrophied brain, and in particular, the hippocampus part of the brain.

This lack of development in the hippocampus portion of the brain is extremely important to school performance because it regulates emotional responses and plays a critical role in how the brain formulates memory and spatial awareness (Dobrin, 2012). The American Psychological Association wrote about the behavioral and emotional problems that children of poverty face. Behavioral issues that impact education often include impulsiveness, difficulty with peer relationships, physical aggression, diagnosis of poor attention, and conduct disorders. Emotional issues often include anxiety, depression, and low self-esteem (APA, 2019). Sound like any of the students you've had in class? You'll see many examples of these deficits in the stories in this book.

11

What this information really means to the educator is that dealing with the unpredictable emotions in classrooms with students of poverty can often be like a roller-coaster ride. Unfortunately, the teacher is not at the controls! Still, even more unfortunate, is that most of these students have little control over their emotions as well. They seem to be as much of a victim of their unpredictable emotions as the teacher.

That's why I often spend a great deal of time talking with students about a variety of emotions. Too often, they arrive at my door with two emotions: happy and mad, and they seem to switch back and forth from one to the other with seemingly no reasoning whatsoever. In fact, I've often asked a student, "What's wrong? Why are you so angry?" Only for the student to reply, "I don't know. I just am!" When they provide us with this response, we've got to accept that, in many cases, they are telling us the truth.

When I've looked at the students in my classroom, I've often felt they were feeling disorganized. Not just with their supplies (even though, that's generally true as well) but disorganized in their way of thinking. They'd have difficulty settling on an answer when asked a question, and a lot of times, seemed to answer a question by making a statement with a question mark at the end, as if to ask, "Is that what I'm supposed to say?"

It's important for us as educators to recognize that much of what we are seeing is not in their control. They cannot control if parts of their brain have not developed to the same degree as others. Especially a part of the brain that's so necessary for school success. Further, they cannot control that they generally come from chaotic homelife situations, and settling into a desk in a structured classroom probably feels like putting on a pair of shoes that are two sizes too small.

If we want to see them experience success, both academically and emotionally, we've got to recognize their deficits, and work towards providing them with strategies and tools that support them in a way that equalizes the playing field for them. It might seem unfair to other students, or it might seem to take a lot of effort, at first; however, the payback will be worth it, I assure you!

These are the students who, when provided with the right support, encouragement, and motivation, will surprise you with how hard they are willing to work to learn and excel.

Working with students of trauma who have difficulty regulating their emotions isn't about making them be good, it's about giving them the power and control over their emotions that make them feel good.

~Belinda Adams, Educator, Author

Are You the Fuse or the Diffuser?

Nope, I am not talking about bombs here. However, if you've ever been on the receiving end of a student who is out of control with dysregulated emotions, it might feel like you've encountered a bomb. It's important to determine if you are the fuse or the diffuser. Part of the problem? Or part of the solution?

To illustrate this point, I'd like to share the story of Jeff. He was a kindergarten student who suffered greatly with anxiety caused by his home situation. Because so many people had walked in and out of his life, up to meeting me, his Mom was the only person he trusted. For the rest of us, little Jeff eyed us suspiciously from his peripheral vision like he was waiting for an attack. When Jeff became upset over issues he felt were overwhelming (his crayon broke or he'd lost his eraser), his first instinct was to run! And run he did, from one end of the school to the other with frazzled me and our social worker hot on his trail. I cannot even recall the number of times, he ran, we followed at a distance that didn't make him feel he was being chased, talked him out of a corner, and walked him back to class.

As time went by, we were nearing October when Jeff began to trust me. I'm sure it had a great deal to do with my predictable routine and structure of the day, and the safety of knowing most of my responses even before I answered. I've learned most of my

Belinda Adams

students who pay attention to what I say generally know the answer they're going to get when they ask the question. Jeff showed his trust in me by making sure I was always in close proximity to him, even when I was delivering instruction. Once I realized it comforted him, I'd offer casually saying, "Jeff, you can come work at my table if you want to keep me company." Jeff liked that, and would often join me at the instructional table once a group left and work at the far corner of the table where I wasn't too close, but not too far away either.

Our relationship became more than co-dependent when Jeff began to rely so much on my presence that I had to let him know if I was leaving my aide in the room while I dashed to the bathroom. Otherwise, he'd look up in a panic and ask where I was. When I went to IEP meetings in the building, Jeff usually ran out of the classroom over some minor situation. Out of exasperation for being called back to my classroom over and over, I asked Jeff one day if he wanted to bring his work and come with me. I told him he could work in the psychologist's office across the hall from where I'd be meeting. Without a word, he packed up his supplies and headed for the door.

When I was in the room, Jeff would look up with wild eyes when something went wrong, such as a broken crayon, and meet my eyes with his. I'd quietly approach and ask what he needed. Often, I'd see his little muscles flexing as he prepared to run but trying hard not to revert to behaviors he knew were not acceptable for school. That's why my immediate attention was needed at the onset of the situation.

While this wasn't the ideal situation in dealing with Jeff's insecurity, I also realized I was the first person he had ever trusted in the school environment, and I wanted to give him time to let that settle into his psyche before trying to put some distance between us.

Somewhere around January, my mom was having surgery, and I needed to stay home with her for a few days. I planned for a substitute that all of the students knew and respected. Except Jeff, who didn't respect or respond to anyone but me. I called his home to let his Mom know I'd be out of school for two days, and to that, she responded, "Oh no! That won't work!" When I asked what she meant, she said that Jeff talked incessantly about me at home, and he was safe at school because of me. She feared that my absence would send him into a tailspin. I tried to assure her that I had a great substitute planned; however, in the end, Jeff and his Mom decided it was best if he stayed home for the two days I would be absent and class work was sent home instead.

Jeff stayed home on days when I had to be out for trainings or absences for the rest of the school year. His Mom said it was much easier than receiving a phone call from the Principal that he had run away or kicked someone trying to bring him back to class, or worse yet, that he was suspended for putting himself or other students at risk with his behavior.

Although Jeff's story sounds extreme, I've had other students over the years with similar reactions. The key here is support. Providing the appropriate level of support is critical for children exhibiting these signs of distress. Sometimes for a student to be successful, you need to start out with a lot of support and gradually allow the student to become more independent as they begin to feel safe and competent.

Students of trauma, such as poverty and other issues, struggle everyday with their involuntary bodily response to run, their "flight or fight" response. What's seems unfortunate to me is that while other teachers have commented on my "magic formula," few have asked how they might duplicate the feeling of safety in their own classrooms for similar results.

Dr. Dan Siegel calls Jeff's response an attachment caused from being "seen." Just as I have practiced over the years, I know my students want to know that I see them, not just in the physical form, but also in the mental sense. To me this means that I let my students know that I understand who they are, I have empathy for their struggles, and I celebrate their successes. This "seen" attachment helps the student develop security and a sense of connection. Further, this connection often leads to problem solving and taking action (Boardman, 2019).

So, I ask, "Are you the fuse? Or the diffuser?" Quite frankly, it's okay to be both because some days we are just human and react before we think. However, if you're the fuse in your classroom more often than not, it might be time to reflect upon your reactions to your students. Sit back, look at them with an objective lens, and determine how you can make them feel safe and secure in your classroom.

Kevin: Leave Me Alone But Don't

I met Kevin the first day of a new school year when I heard a commotion in the hallway before the buses arrived and walked into the hallway to see a pint-sized boy kicking a locker while his mother looked on helplessly. Not knowing that Kevin was actually going to be my student, I knew the situation needed to be addressed. I grabbed a handful of papers off of the table by the door and acted as if I was headed to the copy machine. I walked past Kevin and his mother, seeing her questioning eyes imploring for assistance. Once past, I turned and said off-handedly, "You know the 5th grade lockers don't need a combination to open." Kevin's mother looked at me incredulously as if to say, "Is that the best you've got?" But Kevin stopped kicking the locker and turned his full attention to me.

I took that opportunity to approach Kevin and his mother and introduce myself, "I'm not sure whose class you're in but I'm Mrs. Adams and that's my classroom right there." When Kevin turned to look at the classroom door and then back at me, I asked, "Do you know who your teacher is? Because I can help you find the right classroom." Kevin lifted up his chin and tilted it towards me, and immediately, I knew he was telling me that *I* was his teacher so he didn't need my help doing that.

"Ok, you're with me then. That's great! If you hang on a second, I'll run into the classroom and get your locker number so you can get settled." I could feel Kevin's eyes on me as he watched me walk away and then back. By the way he was looking at me, I'm sure he was waiting for a lecture about kicking lockers. But he wasn't going to get one from me. I'd already stopped that behavior, and certainly didn't want to take a chance to get him started again. Besides, from what I could see, there was no damage to the locker.

When I returned with the locker numbers, I made a big show of explaining that I was running behind schedule and hadn't gotten around to assigning lockers yet. "This is the row of lockers for our students," I said motioning to the lockers across the hall. "Do you have a preference for where your locker might be?" Still eyeing me with uncertainty, he surveyed the lockers and walked over to the one closest to the classroom door and pointed to it. "Great! Let's get your name on that, shall we? What is your name?"

If you hadn't noticed yet, Kevin hadn't said a word throughout this entire scenario; however, we seemed to be engaging in an entire conversation. I opened the locker for Kevin and asked him if he could put his supplies inside while I gave his mom some forms to fill out. He nodded yes and started at the task. I led his mother inside the classroom and again introduced myself.

"Kevin's been upset since this morning when he couldn't find both shoes of the new pair we bought for the first day of school," she hurriedly explained. "That's how come he missed the bus and I brought him to school." "That's too bad," I answered. "I know how excited kids get to show off their new school outfits the first day. Well, we'll get him settled here today and maybe you can locate the shoes today while he's at school." I headed back into the hallway with her quietly following.

That was the first day of school, and unfortunately for Kevin, there were many more days that would begin just as the first day had begun. He often misplaced things at home, missed the bus, and arrived at school angry. It further complicated his frustration when the item he'd lost was an item all the other students had remembered, such as a permission slip for a field trip or money for the school book fair.

Fortunately for Kevin, he had my class for the first half of the day so I was able to handle his raging emotions. Other teachers steered clear of him in the hallways when they saw him stalking by or walked the other way if he was kicking or slamming a locker. I'd had other students like Kevin in previous years, and I wasn't intimated by his behavior. I approached most situations like I had the first time, which was by stating something pretty obvious, but which always drew his attention away from what he was doing.

For Kevin, I realized quickly that his short fuse was caused by two major things: his disorganized home, where items were often lost, and the fact that he was hungry. Once I got this kid settled down for breakfast, he'd eat all of his breakfast and ask for seconds from what other students had placed on the back table that they hadn't wanted for breakfast. I realized if I could get Kevin started eating his breakfast, he was calmed down and ready to move on with his day by the time he had finished.

Kevin had some other triggers besides forgetting things and being hungry. He didn't like to feel stupid or dumb in front of his friends. He rarely raised his hand to answer a question, and found reasons to be out of the room when it was his time to come to reading group, such as an elongated trip to the bathroom or a request to go to the nurse.

I soon realized this was a pattern of behavior for Kevin, and in his own way, a coping mechanism. When I did attempt to ask him to forgo the bathroom until after reading group, he'd use any excuse to become defensive or angry so that he would not have to join the group anyway. After a couple weeks of this, I realized it was better to let him go to the bathroom, and the two of us would read together while the other students were silent reading or on their computers.

Kevin was behind his peers academically as were all of the students in my special education classroom. This was a fact Kevin hadn't noticed yet. He spent so much time and energy trying to hide his own deficits in reading and writing he was unaware of the progress of others.

One day, while Kevin and I were completing the reading group work together, I casually asked, "You know that Marco likes sharks, too?" Kevin looked up from the book he was reading towards Marco and then back to me and shrugged his shoulders as if to say, "Who cares?" I let it drop and we went back to the work we were doing. A few days later, during a writing assignment, I was working with Kevin at the instruction table and noticed that he had the same topic as another student. Again, I passed along this little tidbit of information with much of the same reaction from Kevin. Oh well, I thought.

Most of the students in the class took a wide berth around Kevin because they often heard the banging and kicking of lockers before he arrived in the classroom with an angry face. So he hadn't made any friends in class during the first month of school. My efforts to engage him with other students with similar interests hadn't seemed to make any headway down this avenue either.

I had noticed that several of my students thought he was cool because he could spin a basketball on his finger during gym or folded the paper airplane that went the furthest during inside recess. Still, they didn't take the initiative to get to know him any better and continued to admire his skills from afar.

One day, we were reading, discussing, and writing about camouflage. Marco raised his hand to say that he knew of a shark that could camouflage perfectly with the bottom of the ocean and wait there for fish to eat. "Cool," Kevin whispered before he even realized he had spoken. Marco took this as an invitation to share more about this "cool" shark. Offhandedly, I said, "Hey Kevin, maybe Marco can show you the book where he found this shark when we get into our reading groups." To that, Kevin nodded and Marco grinned because he loved talking about sharks.

That was the day a friendship was born, and those two boys couldn't have been more opposite. You see, Marco was one of the easiest going kids I'd ever had in my classroom. He didn't become upset over lost permission slips or missing the bus (which he hardly ever did). He'd shrug, shoot me a half-smile, and say, "I'll bring it tomorrow, ok, Mrs. A?" Marco knew very well that I always gave extra time for those sorts of things and he had time to get the misplaced item to me or he'd simply ask for another one.

When Marco would see Kevin upset in the hallway in the morning, he'd smile and say, "Dude, what'd you lose now?" as if to say that it wasn't such a big deal. The first time Marco did that, I was fully expecting Kevin to turn around and punch him. Instead, Kevin stopped banging the locker door and walked into class to get breakfast. After about the third time with the same question, Kevin looked up at Marco, smiled, and then, shrugged!

This was a huge step for Kevin. When he began to realize he could let situations drop with a shrug of his shoulders, and knew it wasn't going to become a lecture, he started to use that strategy more and more. As I'd explained more than once, "there's very little in this classroom that should make you that mad because we'll figure it out." It seemed Kevin had finally started to believe that, with the help of Marco.

Kevin also found a reading partner in Marco. The two boys went through every book on sharks they could read in my library and the school library. After scouring the bookshelves, I told them they'd have to come up with another topic, and within a few minutes of discussion, they had settled on a new subject to read about. Kevin found that by working with Marco, the easiest-going kid, his reading mistakes weren't going to be pointed out or ridiculed. Sometimes, I'd hear Marco say, "You know that word is (whatever), Dude? But go ahead." Marco also realized that, when it came to writing time, Kevin had the best ideas and the two of them loved to collaborate on a story.

I encouraged this friendship and often let the boys work together, even though it was independent work time. It soon involved several other twosome groups, but that was okay with me. My rule: I don't care if you work together, but you'd better be working! Most of the students didn't want to lose the privilege of working together and were mostly respectful of my request to work.

Kevin never really opened up to the rest of the class throughout the whole school year. He continued to prefer working with me or Marco rather than sharing out loud in front of the group or joining in a reading group. There were days when he wasn't able to overcome the fact that he had forgotten something at home and lost it completely. On those days, I allowed him to call home to ask his Mom if she might look for it while he was at school. Acting on it seemed to make it easier for him to move forward with his day. On most days, after calling his Mom, he was able to focus better and complete his work.

End of the Day Takeaway

In understanding some of the common characteristics of students of poverty – such as disorganization, no space dedicated for their personal items at home, and lack of food – I was able to find solutions to some of Kevin's triggers. In this way, he was able to reduce his reaction of anger and learn to become part of the learning environment.

For Kevin, it was the little things that made the difference for him:

- *Providing no lectures for bursts of anger or punishments for them either as long as nothing was destroyed.*
- *Allowing him to use the classroom phone to call home to ask his Mom about an item he had left there or misplaced.*
- *Making extra copies of homework and others things, such as field trip forms or announcements about upcoming events, so I could provide him with another copy if he couldn't locate the first.*

- *Assuring there was plenty of breakfast available for him each morning, and even setting some aside if he arrived tardy.*

Kevin was one of those students of mine who stopped by my classroom when he moved onto 6th grade. He'd stop in on his way to the nurse (probably still avoiding reading group!) and ask how my year was going. He always looked around and commented on things like, "You've still got that poster up we made last year about respect. Cool." Then, he would shuffle off to the nurse or lunch. I think, even after leaving 5th grade, Kevin found some feeling of safety in knowing our classroom was still there. He particularly liked knowing that assignments they had completed were still part of my room, even though the class has moved onto the next grade.

As an educator, never underestimate the power you have to help a child make changes in his behavior. For Kevin, it was the little things; things that didn't involve extra time on my part or require me to buy items from my own personal budget. In addition, Kevin needed one thing that didn't cost a penny: giving him some control over situations where he felt helpless. Many children of poverty seek control in the classroom because they often feel they have so little of it at home. Many times, the way in which they seek the control is not conducive to instruction or learning. When Kevin began to feel in control of some of the things in our classroom, such as being able to call his Mom about lost items or working with me or Marco independently instead of a small group, Kevin was able to let go of some of the negative, physical outbursts.

Let's not forget breakfast. I know many teachers who feel that, if a student is tardy for school, they've missed breakfast time and that's the end of that. I'm certain that had been his previous experience with breakfast, and being late and missing the bus almost assuredly equaled no breakfast, thus contributing to his angry outbursts in the hallway upon arrival. Knowing that breakfast would be there for him when he arrived, and extras too, helped Kevin to transition better from being angry about forgetting or losing something to getting on with the rest of the day. I always try to remind myself that, even though breakfast is an inconvenience and sucks up instructional time, for children of poverty, it is instrumental to their day. Many of my students have told me they didn't have dinner the night before or didn't get enough dinner to feel full. Most of them looked forward to breakfast at school, and I could never understand teachers who felt it necessary to take that away from them.

Sometimes, students require big changes or accommodations to be successful. In Kevin's case, it was the small things that made all the difference for him. Never forget that what might seem trivial to you may be a very big deal to students struggling with the trauma of poverty.

Belinda Adams

Crystal: "Keep Outta My Way"

Crystal was a 5th grade student in my self-contained, special education class. She was not new to the district and had been in class with many of the rest of my students since starting kindergarten. She was respected by her peers due to her imposing personality. She was well-known in the school hallways for her ability to get what she wanted by making such a big deal about things that most people gave in just to avoid the scene she would make if things didn't go her way.

That's the demeanor she brought to my class. When I'd ask students to get out their notebooks, she'd sigh loudly and cross her arms across her chest and lean back in her chair. I made the same mistakes as other teachers because I started the year by restating the expectation, making demands, issuing threats of consequences, and losing the battle. I soon learned that Crystal was more interested in derailing instruction and winning the power struggle than she was in learning anything.

Crystal served her consequences: she had lunch detention where the expectation was to complete her work (she did not) and she missed out on preferred activities. None of these consequences made any impact on her behavior whatsoever. If anything, the sequence of events only continued to provide her with more fuel for future power struggles. Her classmates found her impressive, and they secretly reveled in the fact that she was able to avoid work as much as she did and endure the consequences like they didn't matter at all.

One day, I'd had enough. I slammed a book closed I had been reading because I was frustrated with Crystal who was sitting in the back of the room blowing huge bubbles with forbidden bubble gum and popping them as loudly as she could. At first, the students were startled by my outward response of frustration. Then, seeing Crystal's huge bubble expanding unperturbed, a few of them began to snicker. I mean, if I hadn't been the teacher, I'd probably have laughed too because the two of us were making quite the scene. Taking a deep breath, I asked Crystal to stay after class and dismissed the rest of the class to lunch.

When the last student had filed out, Crystal went into her usual posture: crossing her arms across her chest and leaning back in her chair. Rather than explaining that there would be a consequence for her behavior, I pulled the chair out next to her and quietly asked, "Do you have a problem with my class?" I waited (not too patiently) for her to respond, but she didn't. She continued to blow bubbles and pop them loudly while looking at me from the corner of her eyes. "It seems that you don't want to be here, and I'm not sure what we're going to do about it. But this cannot continue." Again, I waited. More bubbles blown and popped. "It's your lunch time you're missing. I can eat in here. I'll wait," I said as I got up and walked to sit behind my desk.

Crystal watched me casually as I pulled open my lunch box and slid out my yogurt and a spoon and quietly began to eat. As I finished my yogurt and reached for a container of berries, she sighed and said, "You mean, you're gonna sit and eat right in front of me?" "Yep," I answered, "I'm waiting to hear what you've got to say." I continued to eat.

Crystal missed lunch with her peers that day because she spent the entire lunch period staring at me with daggers. Yet, she refused to answer my questions. When it was time for Crystal to go to her afternoon class, I made sure she was able to get lunch and eat it at the back of the classroom before joining the class. It wasn't my intention that she go hungry; I was trying to make some headway with her, or the rest of the year was going to be a nightmare.

I knew for a fact that Crystal's behavior was tolerated in most of her classes because the teachers didn't want to engage in a power struggle. And while I agree that no one wins in a power struggle, sometimes they are necessary with students who have learned through years of practice that they can control the climate of the classroom.

The next day, Crystal decided to up her game. Rather than indulging in blowing bubbles, she pulled a bag of potato chips out of her backpack and began loudly crunching them while I was leading a discussion about character traits. Once again, the stunned silence of the students soon turned to snickers. And once again, I dismissed the class and asked Crystal to stay behind. This time, I didn't say a word, I simply began eating lunch at my desk, as Crystal looked on with indignation.

"You just gonna eat your lunch, ain't ya?" she asked angrily. I told her that I was because I could see that she wasn't in the mood to talk. "We are going to need to come up with a solution to our problem because I'm not tolerating your behavior in my class every day," I said. When she turned her back to me and crossed her arms over her chest, I continued, "I'm more than willing to get you to lunch with your friends, but I need to know if you have a problem with my class?"

Quietly through gritted teeth, Crystal responded, "It's not your class. I like yours more than the others." I asked, "Then what's the problem?" Crystal didn't respond. Instead, she continued to sit there silently until it was time for her next class. As before, I made sure she got lunch.

Even after Crystal had missed her third lunch period in a row, Crystal hadn't expanded on her previous statements. I was no further in helping Crystal in the classroom than I'd been before. My classroom environment hadn't improved and my instruction hadn't become any easier due to her constant interruptions with behavior that was not acceptable for the classroom.

I approached Crystal in the hallway before school and asked if she'd step into my classroom. When she arrived, she threw herself into her chair and crossed her arms. I mirrored her body style with my own. She stared open-mouthed at me, but didn't say anything. "Crystal, I've decided that maybe you need a different teacher for language arts and writing. Maybe you'd be happier with another teacher." She sat there stunned. "You know I ain't gonna be happier with another teacher." When I quietly asked why, she snapped, "Because I hate school. There ain't nothing any of you can do about that!" When I didn't answer immediately, she looked at me questioningly, and I dismissed her to her first class.

That day, I decided to do an activity with the class for writing that I hadn't planned upon. I read a passage from a book where a boy described in painstaking detail how much he hated school. Then, I asked the students by a show of hands if any of them could relate to the boy in the story. I wasn't surprised when most of their hands went up. Crystal didn't raise her hand but that was all right because I knew where she stood on the matter.

For the daily writing prompt, I asked the students to work together to make a list or write a few sentences about how school could be better for the boy in the story and them, too. Of course, as I was expecting, I got some pretty silly responses, such as "Teachers should give no work," or "Let us play on the computer all day." However, I did receive some thoughtful responses from several of the students, especially Crystal.

I gained some valuable insights into Crystal's responses to me and other teachers by reading what she had written: "Teachers just be talking at kids all day. 'Do this, do that,' without asking us nothing. I'd like teachers to ask us what we think. It's just too much."

I knew it had taken a great deal of effort for Crystal to share what she had written on her paper. I was able to see through some of her rough façade to the girl who just wanted to feel heard. I realized that I was part of the problem. I needed to reframe my delivery of expectations if I was going to make this school year different for Crystal.

I started by thinking about my week of instruction from a student perspective. I asked myself: Is it loaded with lots of independent reading that requires motivation and perseverance? Are my lessons heavy with delivered teacher instruction or have I built in time for classroom discussion or small group work? I conceded that I needed to make some changes to allow for variety and more student choice in my weekly classwork expectations.

With those thoughts in mind, I made a few modifications to my lesson plans.

Then, I focused my thoughts on Crystal individually. How could I get her "buy in" for our classwork expectations? I thought about how I feel when I take a workshop or class. It's difficult to feel motivated if you don't know where the entire class is going. That's why most instructors offer course objectives or outcomes at the onset of class. Maybe more information might be helpful in motivating Crystal.

On Sunday night, I quickly typed up an outline of my daily lesson plans, including only the steps we would be completing during class. I put a small box next to each for a checkmark when completed. The next day when Crystal arrived, I asked if I could show her something. I handed a quarter piece of paper to her with the 7 or 8 items for the day listed on it. I told her that it helped me when I took classes if I knew what I was going to do so I could know when I would be finished. "I thought you might like to try something like this," and walked away.

Crystal used the checklist system to check off the items we completed in class. Her disrespectful interruptions dropped to almost none and she was diligent about doing most of the classwork when requested. I'm not going to say the system was foolproof because, some days, she just didn't have the tolerance level needed to participate with the class. However, on those days, she didn't blow bubbles or eat potato chips, she sat quietly and waited for class to be over. That was progress in my book!

End of the day takeaway

I succumbed to a huge teacher faux paus with Crystal, and that was letting her know that her behavior was getting to me. My intolerance of her behavior, without attempting to ask why, only solidified for her what she already thought: teachers just talk, they don't listen. I'd like to say that I haven't shown my impatience or frustration with other students throughout the years; however, remembering that most students have stories to tell if we are willing to listen, generally makes me take a deep breath and ask the questions.

There are a few strategies I'd like to highlight about Crystal's story. The first strategy is an effort for me, and one that I consider to be a continual work in progress. The strategy? Wait time. If you noticed when I was asking Crystal questions, I made sure to give her time to respond. It's soooo difficult, let me tell you. I'm well known for having a lot to say, and it can be excruciating to wait for reluctant students to answer my questions. This was also critical if I wanted Crystal to believe that I was not just "talking" at her; I was listening. When I practice wait time, I find that students will answer in one way or another. In addition, I always have to be prepared for the fact that no answer is an answer in their minds.

The second strategy I implemented for Crystal's situation was looking objectively at my lesson plans. I asked questions about how I was presenting the information, assigning the work, and allowing the students to complete the work. By taking a close look at the lessons, I was able to see that there were places for improvement that involved less independent work, more student participation, and choice in work completion.

Finally, the third strategy that I utilized with Crystal was trying to picture the situation from her perspective and applying that perspective to myself. I know how I feel when I don't know where a class/seminar/workshop is going. I feel frustrated and a tad bit anxious. Instructors who provide me with course outcomes are heroes for me, and help guide me through the instruction. It seemed that Crystal benefitted from a similar approach. Yes, it took me a little time to type the outline on Sunday night. I can recall a few Monday mornings when I realized I had forgotten and had to quickly scribble the outline on a post-it. Regardless of how it was presented, it was helpful to Crystal in following the instruction and knowing what was coming next.

Marcus: "Nothing to Say to You"

Marcus was a 6th grade boy in my language arts class. All one had to do was take a look at him and the rage brewing inside of him was clearly visible. In fact, he seemed to radiate anger in a way that made his small body seem constantly poised to fight. When re-directed, he responded by slamming clenched fists onto his desk and shoving his chair back with enough force to often send it turning over or ramming into the desk behind him.

One day, after a particularly volatile class when he became upset for being asked to stop talking with his friend while completing his computer work, I asked him to stay after class. Before I could even speak, he glared at me saying, "I got nothing to say to you!" When I responded that I understood he was angry with me, he continued to glare at the tiles on the floor, appearing to ignore me completely. I said, "I'm not sure how we can have a successful class if you're constantly becoming angry at minor things." He snorted. I continued, "I don't call you out any more times than the other students in this class. It seems you take what I say very personally." "Oh sure," he spat at me, "like it's not?" and walked out of the classroom.

Unbeknownst to me, I seem to have found a nerve in Marcus that I repeatedly struck day after day. I felt as if there was nothing I could say that would help him be productive and have a good day in my class. I spent some time thinking about my exchanges with Marcus, questioning my approach and wondering how he felt he was being singled out. I came up with nothing. Since the first day of school, I had treated him no differently than the other students with regard to re-directs to return to work or requests to stop talking. Somehow, Marcus did not see it that way.

My contentious relationship with Marcus continued into the second month of school, and I realized I was beginning to dread his arrival in the afternoon with the rest of the class. One afternoon, Marcus didn't arrive with the class, and I was surprised because he rarely missed school. I asked if anybody had seen Marcus and one of his friends raised his hand to answer saying, "He got in a fight in the cafeteria at lunch today. I think he got suspended because I saw his dad pick him up." "Oh, that's too bad," was all I could think to say as I started the lesson.

I followed up with the principal after school to get more information and discovered that Marcus had hit another boy in the face during an argument at lunch. Marcus had been suspended for two days. While I was sad about the incident, I have to admit I was partly relieved to know that I wasn't the only one on the receiving end of Marcus' angst.

When Marcus returned, I welcomed him back to class with no acknowledgement from him that I had even spoken. He sat down sullenly at his desk and ignored all of my attempts to engage him in the classroom discussion. When class was over, I asked if he'd stay behind for a minute. Once again, he spoke before I even had a chance to say why I'd asked him to wait. "Whatever you got to say, I don't wanna hear it! I don't need another lecture about not fighting in school because I got that enough and more from my Dad, ok?" I gave him a moment to catch his breath and responded,

"That's not why I asked you to stay, Marcus. I wanted to give you the poster board and the instructions for the project I assigned while you were out. I didn't want any of you to have to buy poster board so I bought one for each of you. Here's yours," I explained as I handed him the poster board and assignment explanation sheet.

Marcus looked a bit embarrassed after his outburst that I just wanted to give him a poster board and not a lecture, but he said nothing. Quietly, I asked, "So your Dad was pretty upset about the fight and the suspension, huh?" With surprising tears in his eyes, he looked up and said, "I got a good whipping and sent to my room without dinner." Feeling at a loss for words, I responded, "I'm sorry to hear that. Mistakes are hard enough to live with sometimes without getting a punishment on top of it." With those parting words, he walked out of the classroom with his head down.

I'd like to say that Marcus and my relationship improved after he shared his story with me, but sadly, it did not. He continued to become upset over minor issues, refusing to accept help when offered, and often walking out of class even before class was over.

However, now, I had a clearer picture of where Marcus' anger was coming from. He was resentful about the power his father exerted over him through spankings and probably verbal expressions as well. I'd learned through years of working with students of poverty that they often feel powerless at home due to their circumstances, and because of this, they attempt to exert control over other aspects of their life, such as school and friendships.

This understanding didn't make it any easier to handle Marcus in the classroom. I tried many different strategies, such as approaching him and whispering a re-direct to get back to work so he didn't feel "called out" in front of his peers. I wrote notes on post-its which I casually placed on his desk, asking him to stop talking and return to work. Still, his response was always the same. He'd become angry, slam his fists on his desk, shove his chair backwards or loudly shout for me to leave him alone.

One day, after an extremely loud outburst from Marcus, I asked him to stay after class. Before he could beat me to talking, I quickly said, "Marcus, this just cannot continue. It's not a good environment for learning." He spat out words at me like rapid gunfire, "Oh yeah, and what you gonna do? Call my house? If my Dad answers, I'm in for another whipping! Will that make you happy?" I looked at Marcus' angry, tear-streaked face for a moment before replying, "No, that's the last thing I want. What I really want is for you to learn in my classroom and not become angry over issues that shouldn't make you angry. I wish you'd tell me how I can help you with that?" He responded, "Nobody can help me. It is what it is. Can I go?" When I nodded my head yes, he left without looking over his shoulder.

Marcus' school year ended with a bang, or maybe, it was a very loud "thud." It was a week before the end of the school, and we were finishing up with class when the Principal arrived at my door with a list of students who had earned the opportunity to attend the school's end-of-the-year field day celebration. She asked if I'd share it with them before they left for their next class because there were permission slips which needed to be returned if students were going to participate. When I read the list of names, and Marcus' name was not on it, he responded by flipping over his desk. It landed with a huge bang on the floor as the rest of the class turned to him with surprised faces. After yelling, "This school sucks," Marcus walked out of class and went to sit in the front office.

I found Marcus there later, not looking at anyone, just sitting there like he had an appointment with the Principal. When I asked what he was doing, he didn't respond, only punched his fist into the palm of his other hand a few times as if to intimidate me from further conversation. Instead, I sat down and quietly said nothing. Finally, he asked, "What are you doing?" When I answered that I was sitting with him, he turned questioning eyes to me. "I know you're upset about not attending field day, Marcus. It's because of those suspension days. You knew that, if any students had behavior referrals in the fourth quarter, they wouldn't be able to attend, right?" He nodded yes. "Then, why are you so angry about it if you were aware?"

Marcus answered with venom: "Because sports is the only thing I'm good at! And that's what field day is all about, and I'm gonna miss out!" I hadn't thought about the situation from that perspective. Marcus was very athletic, and I could understand his disappointment at not having the opportunity to do what he enjoyed. "I wish I could do something, but you know, a rule is a rule." With resignation, he again nodded his head to agree with me, gathered his supplies and went to his next class. Sadly, the school year for Marcus would end on that sour note.

End of the day takeaway

The way that Marcus' father responded when Marcus got in trouble at school was sad. Unfortunately, for children of poverty, punishments are often severe and punitive. I have rarely heard from children of poverty that their punishment taught them a lesson about following the rules, and that's just the problem with punitive consequences. In her book, A Framework for Understanding Poverty, Payne states, "Punishment in poverty is almost always in the negative" (pg. 26). "Discipline tends to be about penance and forgiveness, not necessarily change," says Payne (pg. 107). I've had several students over the years who have reacted just as Marcus did, with anger. Further, his consequences at home did little to curtail his negative behaviors at school.

I've had students who have also responded to punitive consequences at home exactly the opposite. These are the students who seem to want to disappear. They sit quietly, don't' speak up and do their best to stay off of everyone's radar, both teachers and peers. In these situations, it's often these students who are overlooked in the classroom. Because they are quiet and don't cause disturbances in class, teachers may overlook that they, too, are victims of trauma at home. In my experiences, their inability to speak up for themselves and find a voice and some control makes them incredibly vulnerable to peer pressure, bullying, early school drop-out, and other sad outcomes.

In Marcus' case, I was the fuse in our relationship, however unintended it was on my part. For Marcus, it seemed that I represented the group of people in his life who deprived him of control and power. Regardless of my efforts to include him in problem-solving to help or the strategies I tried, Marcus was a victim of a cycle of powerlessness that began at home and touched every aspect of his life. Sadly, at the time, I thought there would be little that anyone could do until Marcus came to that realization on his own.

Looking back, since it's been years that Marcus was in my classroom, I realize that there are strategies I know now that I would have liked to have tried with Marcus. I've learned a great deal about ways I can give a child a feeling of control and power within the classroom setting. I've discovered ways to help a child feel as if they are being offered compromises without degrading the classroom expectations.

For Marcus, I might have tried offering him a time after he completed his work to have 5-10 minutes to talk with his friends during class. In this way, he might have felt I was making an effort to recognize that he wanted to socialize with his friends. Yes, I would have been sacrificing some classroom learning time, but it would have been worth it if Marcus could have been more productive, and less volatile, during class.

Another strategy I would try if Marcus were my student today would be giving him time to cool off before attempting to talk with him after class when he was still angry. I might try meeting with him in the morning before the school day began or offering to meet with him after school before he headed to Boys and Girls Club. By providing him a choice of when we spoke, Marcus might have felt he had some control in our relationship.

Belinda Adams

Chapter 2

Relationship, Relationship, Relationship

"Focusing on relationships and connection plants us firmly in the social world and reduces the tendency to isolate, individualize and pathologize traumatized children and their families."

~Bernie Geary
Child Safety Commissioner, Australia

Teacher: Friend or Foe?

Chronic stress, caused by poverty and other trauma generally equates to children who demonstrate huge distrust of the adults around them. Often, when I've finally gotten my students to talk to me, either through anger or sadness, they've let me know that the adults in their lives frequently make promises they don't keep.

In addition, the adults in their lives are often inconsistent in their responses to their children. Some days, the children can get away with just about anything when parents are in a good mood or distracted with other issues in the home. On other days, children are punished severely for similar behaviors when parents are angry or upset about a home situation.

Lastly, the adults in their life are not "present" for them. I don't mean in the bodily form; I'm talking about a mental presence that builds a trusting relationship.

Having a lack of presence in the classroom can result in student/teacher relationships that are lacking in substance and little or no student commitment to academic success. One article discusses the negative effects of presence by saying that if we don't choose to be "present," we will unconsciously rely or revert to our subconscious programming and perceptions, without realizing we are even doing it (Boardman, 2019). When we react this way, students recognize immediately that we've tuned out, and their individual circumstances and needs are not being met. Not only does that undermine student academic achievement, it changes the students' mood and classroom climate.

A short story which demonstrates how easy it can be sometimes to turn yourself or another peer from a foe to a friend to your students. One year, we had a new psychologist. She was younger and this was her first position in a school environment. Because I worked closely with the related services team, I often answered questions for her or showed her how to complete our special education paperwork. When she first started stopping by our classroom with questions, I'd generally hear 'Who's that?" or "What she doing here?" After she'd leave, I'd tell them her job in the school and explain that I was helping her "learn the ropes" because I'd been around for "about a hundred years." This usually made them smile and they'd return to their work.

About a month into the school year, the psychologist realized that our class took a snack break around 10 am every day. She asked if she could bring her mid-morning snack and sit with our class while we had our break. I enjoyed the adult break and it gave the students a few minutes to talk with one another. Occasionally, they'd include her in a discussion about music or movies because, after all, she wasn't a hundred years old like me.

When two weeks had passed with the same routine, a couple of the students asked where she was when she'd been absent from our snack time for a couple days in a row. At first, I didn't know who they were asking about. Then one of the girls said, "You know. That girl that looks like Ariana Grande." I laughed and explained that she had been out of the building at a training.

When she arrived for snack time the next day, I greeted her and then asked my student if I could share who they thought she looked like. "Sure" was her response. The psychologist was thrilled to hear she resembled a pop star, and said, "Thanks." One day, two of the girls started asking her questions about herself. She was happy they were interested and gladly shared her interests.

A few weeks later, several of the students were practicing for a talent show in my classroom. I'd told them they could use their snack time to practice together. When the psychologist came in, one of the girls quickly waved her over, "Hey, this is the dance you said you know. Come on!" With that, she became part of the dance group, laughing and smiling along with the students.

This story illustrates the power of presence. When the psychologist first started coming in, she was viewed as an outsider by my students. However, just by being present each day, being friendly, and most importantly, opening up about herself, the students had slowly begun accepting her. When they invited her to join their dance, they showed her their highest level of trust by considering her to be "one of them."

Presence. Powerful.

When students feel they do not have a voice in school, it is often demonstrated with a great deal of hostility. Imagine it. In some cases, these students don't have the language skills to share their wants and needs. In other cases, they feel their voices are never heard, even when they are shouting. We have the ability to give them a voice and show them that what they have to say is meaningful.
~Belinda Adams, Educator, Author

The Power of Voice

It's been well documented through numerous studies that children of low-income homes possess less developed vocabulary skills when they reach school age. In fact, one study reported that "children growing up in poor neighborhoods or from lower-income families may hear up to 30 million fewer words than their more privileged counterparts" (Bergland, 2012). Experts agree that word usage is the strongest factor of child vocabulary growth. This deficit in vocabulary places children of poverty at great risk, both academically and emotionally.

When researching this topic, there seems to be several factors behind this documented vocabulary deficit:

- Children hear fewer words from their parents as discussed above.
- Children are exposed to phrases, rather than sentences, which include less complicated word syntax.
- Children hear words and phrases that are often control strategies and directives.
- Children are exposed to home overcrowding.

Let's break these down. When discussing the quantity of words children of poverty hear, we have to consider two elements: the education of the parents and/or primary caregivers and the warmth of the relationship. When adults become parents at young ages (a common occurrence in lower income homes), they may lack the vocabulary themselves and are unable to provide an enriched vocabulary to their children.

According to Payne in her book, *Ae Framework for Understanding Poverty*, she states, "Acquisition of language occurs primarily when there is a significant relationship" (pg. 34). Developing this rich relationship is often difficult in low income homes where parents struggle with the constant stressors of poverty, such as housing concerns and lack of food and money. This parental distress often causes parents to use vocabulary that lacks warmth and instead, sounds authoritarian and less nurturing, such as short commands with little encouragement provided.

In addition to these factors, children of lower income homes are often in homes that are overcrowded with siblings or extended family. This overcrowding affects vocabulary growth because these homes have increased volume levels which minimize the opportunity for quality discussion and allow for little quiet time.

This lack of vocabulary exposure and development greatly impacts a child's ability to learn. In addition to lacking the vocabulary skills to build meaningful learning structures within their brains, students of lower income homes also illustrate delays with language and speech impairments.

Children with these huge holes in their vocabulary often come to school with fewer words to express their wants and needs. Further, they find it impossible to answer questions. Possibly even more detrimental, they cannot engage in a meaningful way with their same-age peers. All of these issues often result in a low threshold of tolerance that causes many children of poverty to lash out or shut down completely. When these children have sat in the seats in my classroom, I've felt my heart break with empathy and been overwhelmed with the desire to help improve their situation.

Belinda Adams

Markise: No Voice

Markise was a first grade boy in my class. When reading his file prior to school, one thing was crystal clear. This was a boy with a great deal of movement in his life. He'd started his school life in our district during preschool, left to attend another district for kindergarten, and had moved back to our district to begin first grade. When I see high transience in a student that young, it usually means I'll see some pretty common characteristics when he arrives.

First, students like Markise are not interested in developing long-lasting relationships because they never know when they're going to move again. Instead, boys like Markise play with whoever is available at recess with little preference for one student over another. Secondly, these students are usually behind their grade level peers in academics and social skills. When students move a great deal, it's difficult for a student's deficits and needs to become visible in the short time the teacher has them in the class nor is their time to plan for meaningful interventions to help them improve academically. Third, they see no value in a student/teacher relationship because they've never had the time to develop one.

Markise was farther below grade level than the rest of the entering first grade students. He couldn't write his name without a model, he recognized about 10 letters of the alphabet (both lower and upper case), and knew numbers up to four. On top of his huge academic delay, this young man also had a huge chip on his shoulder. He made it clear from day one that he wasn't interested in anyone's help.

When it was worktime, Markise would break his pencil in half, toss his papers on the floor, and sit at his desk doing nothing. When approached by either myself or my aide, he'd clench his fists and growl as if to scare us away from coming any closer. Luckily for Markise, we weren't intimated by his behaviors. When Markise was called to the instructional table to work, he'd waste as much time as he could getting there, assuring that the rest of the students in his group were irritated with him when he did finally arrive. While at the table, he'd refuse to engage in any part of the lesson.

My aide and I made it very clear to Markise that we understood that he was struggling to complete the work and we were there to help him. However, the work was going to get done. Whether he did it with the rest of his group, or did it another time (such as during outdoor recess), it was going to be completed that day. To this information, he'd often growl, clench his fists, bang his chair on the floor and often crouch down at the side of the instructional table.

Noticing that Markise seemed to demonstrate only two emotions, anger and indifference, I thought about how I might give him the vocabulary he needed to express himself. Knowing he was behind in language acquisition skills, I realized that the actual appropriate words might take longer to instill. I kept thinking.

What if I made a paper wheel with pictures on it for various emotions? With an arrow that he could turn to tell us how he was feeling? I'd used this strategy before with some success (such as using pictures on desks); however, this would be the first time I'd tried it so soon in the school year with so little trust and rapport with the student. However, I could see that we were making no headway in getting him to communicate his emotions or his needs.

I prepared the wheel using emojis and typed the emotions to go along with each pictured emoji and laminated it and the arrow. One Friday, shortly before dismissal, I knelt down beside him and told him I had something for him. Suspiciously, he eyed me without turning his head. I showed him the wheel, explained the pictures, and told him I thought this might help him tell me and my aide how he was feeling. "That way, you might not need to growl at us" (he was still looking so I smiled). I read the words to him while moving the arrow to each section to show him how he might show "Frustrated," "Angry," "Disappointed," and "Sad."

Markise didn't show any real emotion while I was going through this explanation but I could see he was paying attention. As I started to stand up, I let him know that he would start using the wheel on Monday morning and it would be waiting on his desk when he arrived. As I started to step away, he quietly asked, "Name?" Smiling, I grabbed a Sharpie from my desk and quickly wrote "Markise" in large letters across the top. Satisfied that it was now his, he placed it in the center of his desk and went home.

The first few days Markise had the wheel, he refused to use it to tell us how he was feeling. He continued to growl, bang his chair and desk, and clench his fists. Each time this happened, I'd retrieve the wheel from the safety of his desk where he'd placed it, and move the arrow to a word. "So, it seems like you might be feeling 'frustrated' about this work?" I asked as I turned the arrow to the word "frustrated" and pointed to the emoji. He didn't answer the first five or six times we tried this strategy, and to be honest, we were wondering if it was going to work at all.

One morning, while refusing to go to the instructional table for small group, he was growling and clenching his fists. Once again, I reached inside his desk and asked, "Are you angry about going to small group?" as I turned the arrow to the 'angry' emoji. After what seemed like an eternity, he finally nodded his head, just once, but at least it was an acknowledgement. I asked how I could help him feel better about going to small group. He pointed to small wiggle cushion that was laying on the counter. I asked, "Do you want to take the wiggle cushion with you to small group?" Again, one almost imperceptible nod.

I got the cushion off the counter and asked him to follow me to small group and show me where he was going to sit. When he'd selected his chair, I put the cushion on it, and whispered, "I'm so glad you told me what you needed. I hope this helps you get your work done this morning."

That's how it began. For about two weeks, Markise required an adult to help him in accessing the emotion he might be feeling. Often, we'd have to move the wheel several times before he would reply with a head nod. I took more than one opportunity to introduce him to the word "disappointed" as this is an emotion that many below-level students have not accessed. My aide and I tried to refrain from using "angry" whenever we could, instead using the words "frustrated" or "sad" as a means of showing him there are more emotions than just mad.

I knew we'd finally succeeded in selling Markise on the idea of the emotion wheel when he used the wheel on his own. I had been calling students up to the SmartBoard to answer questions by moving icons to their correct location. Although Markise had had several turns, he started to escalate when the student was called to move the last icon and he knew he wouldn't be getting another turn. Quietly, he reached into his desk, moved the arrow and held up his emotion wheel so I could read "disappointed."

I almost leapt to my feet in celebration, but that surely would have been a misunderstood reaction. Instead, I said, "Markise, I see you are disappointed about not having another turn. How about we start with you tomorrow?" To that, one nod of agreement and a small tilt upward to his lips. After that day, Markise was never far from his emotion wheel, and he took it with him to small groups, music, and gym.

As we neared Thanksgiving vacation, my aide and I noticed that Markise was relying less and less on his emotion wheel. With some coaxing, he'd grunt or mutter "frustrated" or "sad." We'd always acknowledge his emotion by restating it in a sentence and offering choices to help him move forward.

One day, during social lesson, the occupational therapist was in our classroom doing a lesson with the students. Because she worked closely with our class, and had Markise on her caseload, she was well-versed in his emotion wheel and had seen him use it multiple times. However, on this particular day, instead of reaching for his wheel, he raised his hand. Surprised, she first looked at me, then said, "Yes, Markise, how can I help you?" "Sad" was all he said. She was shocked by his use of the word without using the wheel. "Why are you feeling sad, Markise?" she asked. "Didn't call me first. I know that one." Even more surprised but not wanting to miss this opportunity for him to participate, she responded, "I'm sorry. I know you've been paying attention, and I bet you'll know the answer to the next one, too. Want to try?" Markise nodded and smiled.

I recall shortly after the holiday break that a teacher who had been on maternity leave for several months stopped by our classroom when she returned to say hello to the students and my aide and me. When she noticed that Markise was engaged in a conversation with a peer about a certain action hero, she turned questioning eyes to us. We nodded enthusiastically.

After school, she stopped by again to tell us how happy and surprised she was to hear Markise talking! She recalled, just a few months earlier, when he hadn't been saying anything. Giving the vocabulary and an appropriate way to share helped Markise make huge strides in how he communicated.

End of the day takeaway

Most of us who have children who are average in their development of verbal skills might have a difficult time relating to Markise's problem when he arrived. Most likely, we talked with our children about everything, asking about their wants and needs, encouraging their responses, and celebrating each new word they uttered. It seems difficult to imagine a six-year-old boy who struggles with finding the basic words to share how he is feeling. Yet, Markise is not an anomaly. There are more students like Markise than I'd care to imagine. Recognizing their struggles, and the reasons behind them, we can begin to provide them with the skills they need to gain their voice.

Students require vocabulary as a means to learn. They use vocabulary to define a problem, seek more information and solve a problem. Without vocabulary, they have no starting point or method to move forward. However, as educators, we are in a unique position to provide these students with strategies that help them gain vocabulary; first to express themselves, and then, begin to seek more information.

By providing Markise with the words, I was assisting him in making a functional connection between the region of the brain for attachment and the region of the brain that is associated with language. Helping Markise begin to form that connection was the first step in giving Markise his voice.

Belinda Adams

Jaylen: "I Need a Friend"

I'll always remember the day I first took notice of Jaylen. I already knew who he was. Many teachers in our school had spoken about him over the course of describing their awful day. Everyone at school had heard of Jaylen due to his explosive behavior and knack for avoiding most classwork. In fact, thinking back, I realized that I had never heard one good thing about Jaylen.

On that morning, I was at my door early to greet students as they arrived. I looked up quickly at the clashing sound of a locker being hit and witnessed the arrival of an obviously angry young man. Jaylen marched down the hall hitting each locker as he went with the assistant principal following close behind, as they proceeded to the office. I never discovered what event had caused such anger that morning that evoked such a volatile response from such a tiny kid because Jaylen must have weighed 10 pounds less than his grade level peers.

Later that day, I stopped by the in-school suspension room to pick up some papers from the supervisor there. I wasn't surprised to see that Jaylen was there, more than likely for his morning behavior in the hallway. No longer angry, he was sitting quietly at a desk in the corner of the room, facing the wall. Looking at those slumped shoulders and feeling as though this young man could use a friend, I casually said "Hi" as he glanced up when I entered the room. He quietly said "Hi" in return and turned his gaze back to the wall in front of him.

As it turned out, a few days later, I learned that Jaylen was in the classroom next to mine with a teacher who was known for her strict rules and sharp responses. On the following mornings, I made a point to say "Hi" to him when I saw him at his locker. He'd always respond with a quick, respectful "Hi" and very little eye contact.

A few weeks later, I was in my room waiting for one of my students who had earned a reward for completing a certain level on his math program. I wanted to make sure I recognized DaShawn's efforts because it was about three months of work. All students who completed the program could choose a small toy or a candy bar to acknowledge their efforts and achievement. I hadn't had time earlier in the day to let him choose his reward and had told DaShawn to stop by after school on his way to the Boys and Girls Club. I was surprised when he showed up with Jaylen. As it turned out, the two boys were cousins and always walked to Boys and Girls Club after school together. Feeling bad about giving DaShawn a candy bar in front of Jaylen, I offered one to Jaylen. I was surprised when he said no but asked if he could have the crunchy granola bar sitting on my desk instead. He must have sensed my dismay because he went on explain that there were 2 granola bars in the package, and he would be able to give one to his sister when he got home. "Just in case we are were still hungry after dinner," he added as if that explained everything.

After the boys left, I sat pondering this new information I had learned about Jaylen. Because I'd never heard anything good about him from any adult in the building, I wondered how he could be so thoughtful to think of his sister and turn down a candy bar for a granola bar and no one knew this about him?

Still thinking about Jaylen and his sister, I wrote myself a note to bring a box of granola bars to school the next morning. When I arrived at school the next day, I put one on my desk to remind myself to say something to Jaylen. When I saw Jaylen at his locker that morning, I told him I had an extra granola bar he could have if he stopped by after school. He nodded his head with a smile and walked away.

Within days, Jaylen and I had a routine. He'd drop by my classroom following school and pick up his granola bar and thank me on his way to Boys and Girls Club. During these brief visits, Jaylen and I developed a relationship. He trusted me to be there, waiting with the granola bar, and trusted that there were no lectures or stipulations that went with the granola bar.

Often, when Jaylen came in, we would spend a few minutes, just chit-chatting. He would ask about my son or my weekend. I'd ask about his sister and his daily point sheet. Most days he would tell me he didn't make his points and guiltily stare at the floor. Jaylen told me he tried to be good, but sometimes, he didn't have a pencil and would get in trouble for asking the girl next to him if he could use a pencil. Other times, he admitted, he wasn't listening and didn't know what to do. No matter how hard he tried, he was always out of his seat for something or playing with something.

Jaylen never lied about his behavior. Or made excuses. He would deliver the news of his point sheet and the situations that had happened as if he felt the outcome was out of his control, and that regardless of how hard he tried to follow the rules of the classroom, he never seemed to measure up.

One afternoon as Jaylen was in my room talking with me after school, his teacher stomped angrily into the room. Evidently, she had noticed Jaylen was coming into my room every day and she wasn't happy about it. With little thought about how she appeared or sounded, the teacher screamed at me, telling me that Jaylen didn't deserve a treat. She informed me Jaylen had only made his points one day that week and his behavior shouldn't be rewarded with candy from me.

Answering more calmly than I felt inside, I responded that I never gave Jaylen candy. Quickly, she turned to Jaylen and demanded to know what he was doing in my room. Jaylen said we were just talking; I was his friend. She looked at me, with veins bulging in her neck and exclaimed that Jaylen did not deserve to be in my room talking and I needed to forbid him to visit. I said nothing as she stomped out, but I had no intention of telling this kid he could not stop by my room to visit, for a granola bar, or anything else he needed!

A couple days later, Jaylen appeared after school sobbing. I asked what was wrong, but he was crying too hard to talk. Finally, he calmed down enough to say that he wouldn't be at school the next day because he was suspended. Through sobs, he said, "It ain't true. My teacher hates me. She says I don't do anything right." With a little more coaxing, he told me the teacher said he was wandering the halls when he should have been in class. By now he had calmed down a little, and through sniffles, said all he did was say hi to Mrs. Roberts (her room was almost directly across the hall from his room and on the way back from his locker).

Feeling angry at the mistreatment of this student but still not wanting to put another teacher down in front of her student, I said that it was tough to feel that way. I finished by reassuring him that I liked him, and Mrs. Pirog liked him, and Mrs. Roberts, too. To this, he nodded his head with resignation that he'd still be suspended the following day. Probably the one thing that saddened me the most was that while I was trying to console this student, the one thing I couldn't say was I was pretty sure he was right – his teacher didn't like him.

I would never tell him; I was pretty sure his teacher despised him. You see, the verbal lashing I'd received a few weeks earlier about him not deserving a treat had not been the last conversation I had with Jaylen's teacher. She had taken other opportunities to tell me how inappropriate it was for me to be nice to Jaylen when he didn't deserve anyone being nice to him. For fear of becoming unprofessional with a colleague, I'd ended those conversations by merely walking away.

It took a great deal of restraint for me not to cry that afternoon with Jaylen. I know that life just isn't fair, but every kid deserves to have someone who likes him. And Jaylen deserved it; not on the basis of his behavior, but on the basis of being a kid.

Can you imagine the psychological damage done to a 7, 8, 9-year old who believes no adult likes him? Can you imagine this kid each new school year, with high hopes that maybe this year will be different? Maybe his teacher would like him? Maybe this would be the year he would feel safe at school? Maybe this year he would feel he was welcomed and belonged in his classroom? No child should have to ponder these questions.

End of the Day Takeaway

Although he demonstrated it in a different way, Jaylen was much like Markise. He, too, felt he had no voice, or ability, to express his thoughts and feelings. By listening to Jaylen, he gained confidence in his voice.

Many of us have been in the position – we've had a kid in our class we just couldn't connect with, maybe even a student we didn't like. Generally, this is because the kid is making our lives miserable. Take Jaylen for example: a wiry, little hyperactive kid, who couldn't stay in his seat. And I'll admit I've had many students who have challenged my belief that every child has a special gift or talent.

The key for the Jaylen's of the world is to develop a relationship with them. I can just imagine some teachers rolling their eyes, thinking it can't be that simple. But it is. Do you know why? Not because it changes the kid; because it changes you. Once you begin to get to know the student, it's easier to really like the kid. Forming a relationship changes your views about him.

Take a moment and reflect on your most difficult student. I bet, if asked, you'd have no problem making a long list of all of this student's characteristics that had made teaching him impossible and brought disruption to your classroom. I'm going to challenge you to do the opposite. Close your eyes, and try to think of the good characteristics of this child. Write a list. If you've spent any time watching this student at all, I'm sure you can find something "good" about him; perhaps, he is loyal to his friends, or a good athlete, or a creative artist. This is the kind of activity that brings about positive change in your classroom, both for your student and you.

In the beginning, you will probably have to be pretty creative to come up with anything. For Jaylen, it was his kind heart and generosity to his sister; a heart that would forego a candy bar so he would have something to share with his little sister. Another positive character trait was Jaylen's honesty. While his ADHD may have prevented him from following the rules, he admitted that he broke the rules. Both of those characteristics could be the foundation for a great student/teacher relationship that could lead to better classroom behavior and learning.

When you change how you think about the student, it will change the way you treat him, and ultimately, the way you feel about him. In return, the student will respond positively. I've seen it happen, year after year, in my classroom. It's not always easy, and some students take a great deal more effort than others. However, it certainly beats the alternative of disliking the child for an entire school year while enduring the negative behaviors in class. And your attitude change provides this student with hope for a better year ahead of him.

Belinda Adams

Analee: "I Was Hungry"

When I was teaching at the elementary school level in a primarily Hispanic school, it was not uncommon for me to have over 25 students in my classroom. One year, I had 31 students; 19 girls and 12 boys. A great deal of activity occurs in the classroom with that many students, and it's nearly impossible to keep everyone still. That is, until my students were introduced to read-aloud time after lunch. Many of my first-grade students had never had a story read aloud to them, let alone a book with rich illustrations that was selected just for them. I'd go to the public library on weekends and select a read-aloud for each day of the week for the next two weeks. That time was revered by my students, and there was little that could distract them during read-aloud time.

There were many people who entered my classroom during various parts of the day to hear it sounding like a huge beehive with just about as much activity, too. Because there was so many of them, I often allowed them to make room wherever they could to complete their work. It wasn't uncommon to find small groups laying on their stomachs working and others using lapboards and leaning against the walls.

My principal often joked that he never knew how he was going to find us, and walking towards my desk, often required him to step over children, around children, over a few unfinished puzzles they had begged me to save, just to have a word with me. One day, I asked him, "Is my classroom too loud?" He chuckled and said, "Well, there *are* 31 of them in here. Besides, the noise I hear is excited children talking about the work they are doing with one another. That's the greatest sound a Principal can hear!" I took that as an invitation to continue with what I had been doing.

Analee was a particularly bubbly, energetic girl. She was very smart, finished all of her work, offered to help others, and spent time each day "playing teacher" by putting student homework into their cubbies. In addition to her busy demeanor, she was also very outspoken about what was on her mind. "This homework is too easy" or "I bet the boys aren't going to like this homework sheet because of the flowers" were not uncommon observations for me to hear while she was helping me. When she was helping other students, she always assumed a teacher attitude, often pausing after asking a question and pointing out when someone needed to sharpen their pencil or clean up their supply box. All of this was taken in by her fellow peers without exception.

One day, while stamping the word "Homework" on the pages before stuffing them into cubbies, she casually said, "My teacher last year didn't like that I finished first all of the time." I wasn't sure what to say so I didn't say anything. She continued, "He would give me another worksheet and another one until all the kids were finished." I paused, then said, "Oh, how did you feel about that?" She answered, "Annoyed, and a little bit mad. He didn't listen when I tried to tell him." I explained to Analee that sometimes teachers give extra work to their smartest students so they can keep learning. She snorted as if to say she wasn't buying that story. Soon, it was time to go home and the conversation was dropped.

I started out the school year having my 31 students line up single file as I had done in previous years. This posed some challenges because I couldn't keep the whole class in my view after I'd turned one corner with half the class, the rest of them had yet to make it around. Often, it was from the rear of the line that I'd hear giggles and whispering. I'd try to return to the corner to give them the peace sign which signaled for them to be quiet in the hallway; however, when there's 31 one of them, it was often hazardous to leave the front of the line to check on the back.

One day, as my students and I were headed out of my classroom, the kindergarten teacher next door appeared at her classroom door to stare stonily at us. I wondered if we'd been too noisy lining up but didn't have time to ask. The next day, the same thing happened when we were lining up for music. Hmmm? I made a mental note to stop by after school to ask if we were too loud and disrupting her classroom. However, I forgot to speak with her after making copies and preparing my room for the next day.

On the fourth day of her appearance at the door, I was really becoming paranoid. I reminded the students repeatedly as we were lining up that we needed to be respectful of the other classrooms, and I'd thought we were doing a pretty good job of that. When we were returning from music to go back into my classroom, there she was again standing in her doorway.

After school, as I walked by, she came running towards me, talking quickly and angrily in Spanish. I don't think she even realized she was speaking entirely in Spanish – that's how upset she was. When she took a breath, I asked, "English please." She stopped, took a breath and started to laugh. Finally, she said, "I've been keeping an eye on your class." To that, I responded, "Yes, I've noticed. What's going on?" She explained.

"Someone in your class is stealing my students' artwork off of the walls," she said. My face must have said it all because she led me out of her classroom to point to the artwork attached to the wall near her classroom door. She continued, "I wondered where all of the Cheerios were going that my students used to decorate their names. Finally, I realized that someone in your class must be tearing them off when you walk by because they aren't falling off onto the floor or I'd see them." I was speechless at first, and then I started to shake my head in disbelief. "I'll get to the bottom of it tomorrow and let you know what I find out."

The next day, after read-aloud and before we lined up for music class, I told them I needed to have a serious conversation with them. Being that it was rare for me to use a stern tone with them, they all turned solemn faces towards me. I explained what the kindergarten teacher had shared with me and told them I was disappointed that someone in our class would be disrespectful to another student's work. "How would you feel if someone was destroying your work in the hallway?" No answer, just more solemn faces. "Can anyone tell me why this is happening?" No one said a word. Most of them tried their best to keep looking forward; however about five of them turned to look directly at Analee. Surprised that Analee would destroy someone else's work, I asked if I could talk with her a few minutes before she went to music. I had another teacher walk my class to music and I asked Analee to sit by me so we could talk.

Before I could get a word out of my mouth, Analee blurted, "I'm sorry. But I was just hungry!" I was speechless as I stared at her doubtfully. Before I could answer, she continued, "It's so long after lunch, Mrs. Adams. I just saw the Cheerios and ate one and the next day I ate more than one." I was still too stunned to speak. Finally, I asked, "You know those Cheerios have glue on them? That's how they're sticking to the paper." Now it was her turn to be speechless before she said, "You're upset, aren't you? Am I gonna die from that glue?"

I answered, "Nope, I'm not mad and you're not going to die from the glue on the Cheerios. You didn't feel sick after eating them, did you?" When I received a negative bob of her head, I continued, "That glue is made for kids to use so it's not going to kill you if you eat it. It's just probably not that good for you." When she looked up at me and said, "I'm very sorry. How can I fix it?" I responded, "Well, first, I'd like you to apologize to Mrs. Achoa next door. And then, tomorrow during lunch recess, we are going to glue Cheerios back on the papers, ok?" She nodded and smiled.

On our way to music class, Analee had recovered her happy spirit and was skipping a bit as she walked. "It's really a good thing no one else was hungry, isn't it, Mrs. Adams?" With that, she walked into music class.

End of the day takeaway

When teachers take the time to develop relationships with their students, they are generally pretty honest about situations which occur because you've already taught them to be proactive about using their voice. Further, when they know that your consequences are fair and not punitive, the students don't worry about sharing the truth and asking how they can make things better. Even with students as young as first grade, it's possible to teach them that most things can be "fixed." That's why Analee asked what she needed to do. She'd internalized what I'd been teaching; everyone makes mistakes and it's our responsibility to make things right when we do. I also let Analee know that next time she was that hungry, she should let me know and we would find her a snack.

Needless to say, it was a comical story when I informed the kindergarten teacher how and why the Cheerios had disappeared from her students' artwork. She laughed and said, "Only your class, Mrs. Adams, only your class."

It was that day that I changed my line-up procedure. Boys in one line, girls in another. That way, I could see the entire line at all times, even after we'd turned a corner.

Dan Siegel
The 4 S's of Attachment

Throughout this chapter, I've talked a great deal about the relationship between teacher and students, and in particular, students of poverty. You've read some stories that have resulted in great outcomes from positive relationships, and conversely, you've read how a negative relationship can be detrimental to a child of poverty.

Dan Siegel's model connects these stories together with the concept of the 4 S's of Attachment. While these elements are often associated with parenting, we have to remember that, for many of our students, we are the closest positive parent model in their lives. This is especially true if children have not formed a positive attachment to their parents or primary caregivers due to excessive stress in the home or other negative factors. When that is the case, we've got to work at developing the elements of the 4 S's if we have any chance of making a connection with these children.

The 4 S's of Attachment are Safe, Seen, Soothed and Secure:
- **Safe** – The child feels a sense of safety; physically, emotionally and relationally.
- **Seen** – The child feels "seen" when the adults around him are attuned to what's going on inside of them. For children to feel seen, we need to focus our attention on their inner feelings, thoughts and memories, and remember to look at what's going on beneath the behaviors we are witnessing.

- **Soothed** – The child learns, with support, that there will be difficult times in life; however, the adults are present and will be there if the child needs them.
- **Security** – As the child consistently experiences the feelings of safe, seen and soothed, the result is a feeling of security. Security results from the adults' predictability; children know the certainty that they can count on the adults in their lives unconditionally.

The good news of the 4 S's comes to light when Siegel reminds all parents, caregivers, and educators that children do not need perfection. As adults and human beings, we will always make mistakes. The difference for the child occurs when we acknowledge our mistakes, such as harsh words or a punitive criticism, apologize and repair the relationship. For those who wonder if children need to talk about their emotions, Siegel reminds us that children feel seen when we pay attention to their emotions – both positive and negative – and help the child to recognize the emotions and talk about them.

Although there are parents who may want to protect their children from all harmful experiences, Siegel reminds us that is unreasonable. The key to children feeling soothed is for them to experience a "deep awareness" that they will not go through these situations alone.

According to Siegel, the results of our efforts will culminate into a "whole brain child;" a child that responds to the world around her with an attitude of "security, demonstrating more emotional balance, more resilience, more insight and more empathy" (Siegel, 2020). The 4 S's definitely provide teachers with the right ingredients to increase academic achievement and build solid emotional regulation.

Belinda Adams

Chapter 3

Teacher or Lecturer?

Good educators love their students first and foremost.
They empathize with their student's failures and
celebrate their successes.
Good educators instill perseverance and hope for the future.
~Belinda Adams, Educator, Author

Recalling My College Lessons

I learned many valuable lessons while attending college to become a teacher. Being that I was older than the rest of my classmates because I already had a degree in psychology and had been in the business world prior to starting college, I already had some of a teacher's most valuable assets: communication skills and perseverance. However, I still had plenty to learn about different ways for addressing student academic deficits and discovering there is no "one way" to teach children to learn.

One of the key philosophies I learned was that, as an educator, it's very easy to stand in front of the class and teach. Most of us have communication skills and vocabulary that drives our families insane, so talking about subject areas generally comes very easily to us. However, teaching is more than delivering information. Students really begin to learn through exploration and application of the skills you've taught them.

For example, I experience huge excitement when one of my students can explain how to do something to another student. Sometimes, I'll ask them to out of frustration because the student I'm trying to instruct is really struggling with my word choice. Other times, ambitious students will jump in saying, "Can I show him how to do it?" To which I always answer, "I'd love that!"

The key phrase I learned in college: "It's better to be the guide on the side than the sage on the stage." These days, I think of that as, "Do my students view me as their teacher? Or their lecturer?" The answer to that question in each of their minds can mean the difference between what they learn or do not learn.

Alexis: "I've Got This!"

Alexis was a second-grade student of mine. She was a small girl, but what she lacked in size, she made up for in personality. Alexis was passionate about lots of things and wasn't afraid to share her views with others. In fact, for an 8-year-old, Alexis was very well informed on topics such as how to make the tallest Lego tower and why the liquid detergent Dawn will get oil off of ducklings. Very eclectic, I know.

Because Alexis knew so much, she was often butting into conversations where she was not invited, which made many of her classmates upset. It wasn't uncommon for Alexis to be involved in more than one heated conversation per day, and it usually took a refereeing adult to bring the yelling to a halt. It didn't seem to matter how many chats I had with Alexis about waiting to be asked to join a conversation, it appeared that she just couldn't resist the urge to share all that pent-up knowledge.

I tried to speak with Alexis's mother about the situation, explaining that she was alienating herself from her friends at school. Her mother was very unsympathetic, saying that she had the same problem at home, and just sent her to her room and closed the door. That got me thinking. Maybe the reason Alexis couldn't resist the urge to join in uninvited was because she wasn't given any kind of audience at home.

I asked Alexis a few days later where she learned all of the information she shared in class. "My grandma," she answered. "She watches me when my Mom's at work, and she lets me watch The Learning Channel or look up stuff on her tablet." I asked, "Does your Grandma listen when you talk about what you watched?" "Nope," was her casual response as she walked away.

I started wondering how I could give Alexis a voice in the classroom to share what she knew that didn't interrupt the other students when they were talking about other topics? I'd done Show and Tell earlier in the year, and I didn't feel like that would be a good forum for Alexis as I was sure she'd jump in with some fact or tidbit of information about everyone else's items.

I tried to focus on Alexis's most frequent points of conversation. That got me nowhere because Alexis pretty much had something to say about everything. Next, I looked around the room and thought about times during the day when having a second set of helping hands, or a voice, would be helpful. I realized that logging onto our computers was usually a nightmare each and every day.

One student would experience problems with logging in while another forgot her password and needed me to look it up while still others were struggling to get to the right site to start their work. I asked Alexis how she'd feel about being the "teacher" during morning login on our computers. She was elated and answered, "You mean, I get to help them and tell them how to do stuff?" To that, I answered, "You bet!"

I didn't say anything to the other students about Alexis's new classroom responsibility. I knew how they felt about her butting in, and didn't want to set this new venture off on the wrong foot. When the first student raised her hand to say she was having an issue logging in, I walked over to assess the problem. I could see that Alexis was trying her best to wait to be asked to join in the problem-solving mission. When the second hand went up while I was still working with the first student, I said, "Alexis, do you think you could help Michael over there? I'm still busy over here." She nearly flew to Michael's side and asked, "What's up?" When she finished with him, another hand had gone up, and I gave her the same direction. Within minutes, Alexis and I had everyone logged onto their computers and working quietly. Alexis sat down at her desk with a satisfied sigh.

After several days of the same procedure, the students started raising their hands and asking for Alexis to help them. She gladly agreed. One day, while the students were doing research on a Google project they were completing for media class, several of them were getting frustrated with how to spell things correctly in the search bar to locate the pictures they wanted. There was a great deal of sighing, moaning, and a few hand slaps on top of their desks as they expressed their displeasure at not being able to find what they were looking for. When Alexis stepped over to help one boy, I heard her saying, "You really don't have to spell it right all the way. You see, if you just start typing, something will pop up. You just have to make sure you have the right first letter sounds." Other students who had overhead Alexis tried her idea, and the students were happy to finally make some progress.

Once Alexis became known as the computer "gen-e-us," the students couldn't wait to hear her ideas about search topics or other interesting facts she had found on the computer. It wasn't uncommon for one of the students to ask during free time on the computer, "Hey Alexis, where'd you find that site that has the music you make from the letters in your name?" Alexis was always eager to share what she knew.

Everyone, including me, learned a valuable lesson from this experience. Alexis realized that there were people who were willing to listen to her ideas and ask for her help when she *listened* to what they needed. The students learned that Alexis *really* knew a lot of stuff, and she could be helpful and lead them to fun sites on the computer. And me, I recognized the value of empowering one student provided her with an acceptable outlet for her knowledge and allowed her to feel like a valuable part of our classroom.

End of the day takeaway

As teachers, I think it's frequently hard for us to delegate because we often get accustomed to doing things on our own. It's common to get caught in the trap of running ourselves ragged each day while we try to meet the needs of all of our students. Yet, in Alexis's case, asking for her help with the computers not only helped me, it helped her and the other students, too.

Empowering Alexis with a job that allowed her to share her knowledge without offending her friends or butting into their conversations permitted her to share so much information with her classmates and improved her self-esteem and her relationship with them.

Christian: The Great Outback

Each year, at our very culturally diverse elementary school, we would hold a cultural fair in our building. Every classroom selected a country, studied it, and decorated the classroom showcasing the characteristics of that country. I always chose Australia because each year, towards the end of the year, the first-grade classes did a poetry unit which included one of my favorite poets, Mem Fox, who was from Australia. It worked out that the cultural fair coincided with the poetry unit.

Many of my students had never traveled outside of Illinois for family vacations. Some of them had visited relatives in Mexico but few of them had seen anything beyond Illinois and Mexico and had never heard of a place called "Australia." It was great fun introducing them to this island, learning about the country, its inhabitants, and the Australian lingo. Actually, the lingo was my favorite part.

One year, I had a very inquisitive boy named Christian. He liked to learn about everything! And the fact that we were learning about another country surrounded by water was very appealing. Even though Christian was inquisitive, he quickly became "bored" with concepts and would often sit sullenly at his desk if asked to make a minor correction to his work. He'd get excited about a topic, and quickly discover, in his mind, that it was just "too much work" to continue to develop his skills further. Because of his inconsistent work habits, Christian had fallen behind some of his grade level peers in reading and math skills. This lack of perseverance could result in Christian falling further and further behind as he advanced in grades and the academic expectations become higher, if he didn't find some self-motivation.

In preparation for the cultural fair, our class read poetry and other literature; we studied the people and the animals. We decorated our entire classroom to look like Australia. Each year, it was a little bit different, but always great fun … for the students and me!

This particular year, Christian's curiosity about everything Australian made the event even more enjoyable. We made didgeridoos, a wind instrument of northern Australia. The students traced one another and created a small tribe of Aborigines, including children. Christian, who liked animals, created a small herd of kangaroos and their babies, some in pouches and some out. We made boomerangs and practiced throwing them outside. Although, for some reason, none of them came back to them.

Before we even knew what happened, the entire classroom had been transformed into the Australian Outback and the students couldn't have been more pleased. One wall was lined with Aborigines; another wall was filled with kangaroos and dingoes; and the other walls reflected the artwork of Australia, both past and present.

During this time of transforming our classroom, I was waiting for the usual response from Christian that he was "bored" with what we were doing. However, thus far, he had not. Throughout the weeks of preparation, we'd been learning the

Australian lingo, and the students were getting pretty good at the Australian accent, especially Christian. Once he learned the phrase, "G'day Mate," he never said "Hello" to another person for the last month of school. And the more lingo he learned, the more he enjoyed it. One day, during math class, I noticed he had stopped working. I approached him and asked him if he needed any help. Without hesitation, he looked up at me and said, "Sheila, this boy is just knackered." I started smiling and then laughing because he had just said, "Girl, this boy is just too tired."

Finally, the day of the cultural fair was upon us! My class was excited, and they couldn't wait for the first visitors to arrive. As was the tradition, each classroom in the school took turns visiting the countries and completed a scavenger hunt worksheet as they completed their tour. With each class arrival, it was Christian who greeted them at the door with a huge smile saying, "G'day Mates! Welcome to Australia." Other students demonstrated how to play the didgeridoos, others introduced them to the Aborigines or the kangaroos and dingoes. Still, others were interested in showing off the artwork they had completed.

As the afternoon waned on and the classroom visits were coming to a close, most of the students were exhausted from their efforts and were quietly coloring at their desks. When a distinguished looking man in a suit appeared at our door, it was Christian who jumped from his chair and greeted the man saying, "G'day Mate! Welcome to Australia." Needless to say, the Assistant Superintendent was thrilled with the hearty welcome to Australia and asked if Christian might show him around.

Christian couldn't contain himself. He spoke about every detail of our Australian Outback, from the "bush" to the "roos and joeys" and to the grill where they'd eat "shrimp on the barbie."

Never once did he drop his Australian lingo and it was more than amusing to our visitor.

When asked how the day had gone, he responded, "For most of us blokes, it's been a good day. The sheilas liked showing off our artwork. Right now, we're feeling pretty knackered!" The Assistant Superintendent couldn't hold back any longer and started to chuckle at Christian's full-out Australian vocabulary.

As I approached them, I thanked Christian for his thorough tour of Australia and told him he could go back to his seat if he wanted. Before he walked away, he said over his shoulder, "See if the bloke would like my didgeridoo as a souvenir of his trip to the Outback." Again, more chuckles from our visitor and me, and he did leave with a 3-foot, cardboard didgeridoo for a reminder of his visit.

End of the day takeaway

What's there to say? Allowing my class to take over our classroom and transform it into the Australian Outback was a delight to watch. Yes, it was a bit messy for the better part of a month. Yes, I might have made the Aborigines taller and the roos shorter; however, it was their creation and their pride in what they had accomplished could be seen clearly by all who entered our room.

As for Christian, it appeared as though he learned a valuable lesson about seeing something through from beginning to completion. His total "buy-in" about the Australian Outback and his excitement over the lingo not only inspired him to learn more and more, it also encouraged his classmates. I hoped this was just the beginning of Christian's excitement and follow through in completing what he started at school.

The students voted to keep our classroom as the Outback until the end of the school year. Very few of them kept up the lingo, except Christian who had developed quite a fondness for calling girls "sheilas" and letting me know when he thought he was too "knackered" to work. Many of them left on the last day of school with a rolled up kangaroo or a cardboard instrument. As for Christian, I'm sure it is an experience he recalls to this day!

Belinda Adams

Jesse: "It's a Tar-a-dactle"

I love teaching summer school! It's usually an opportunity to engage in some fun, non-curriculum specific activities because so much of my school year is dedicated to pacing guides and deadlines. One year, I planned for all of us to be Storm Chasers, and I designed all of the curriculum (math, reading, writing, social studies and science) around the weather. The students had a blast doing cloud math, and tornado reading and earthquake writing.

Another year, I decided that the theme for summer school would be Paleontologists and we'd spend the four weeks of summer school looking for dinosaurs. Because I had 6 boys who loved dinosaurs in my summer school class, this theme was terrific for them! As I had the previous year, I designed the lessons and subjects around different dinosaur activities, including fossils, dinosaur identification and learning the Paleontologists' "tools of the trade."

Fortunately for me, I was helped with the activity planning for this summer school theme by a retired teacher who was well known for her creativity. She thought up some great activities, such as looking at fossils under a microscope, building tiny dinosaurs from a block set she'd purchased, and of course, digging for dinosaurs. She had located a recipe online for mixing sand with water and some other things that would harden the sand when it

95

was baked. She created about 15 different pans, some containing tiny dinosaurs, dinosaur bones and rocks with fossils. It was going to be a great experience.

One boy, in particular, was obsessed with dinosaurs. He'd spent the week between the end of the school year and summer school researching dinosaurs, watching Jurassic Park 10 times, and assembling dinosaur Legos. Yes, Jesse was ready for summer school.

I had planned that Thursdays would be "dig days," meaning that we would complete our research and observations of fossils and bones Monday through Wednesday. Thursdays would be dedicated to digging up dinosaurs. The prerequisite was that the students needed to have completed their work the first three days of the week if they were going to participate in the "dig". This was an incentive for most of them, but especially for Jesse. He raced through his work quickly, and often had to be sent back to finish the rest of the page or add some punctuation to his sentences.

Often, during the first week of summer school, Jesse had to politely correct me when I called a dinosaur by the wrong name or mispronounced the name. After the first week, when someone would ask, "Which dinosaur is that?" I'd say, "Let's ask Jesse." He was happy to tell them all about the dinosaur, including their diets in such extreme detail that someone would usually say, "Gross."

One issue with Jesse was that he only wanted to study what he wanted to study, which in this case, was dinosaurs. While there were many other topics for paleontologists, Jesse would voice his disinterest with grunts of dissatisfaction or complete his work with little regard to the quality of it. He required frequent recaps that paleontologists study a great deal more things than just dinosaur bones and reminders that work completion was necessary for everyone.

Getting all of the boys to complete their work that first week was a challenge. One of the boys kept reminding me that school was over as if to say that real work was out of the question. Another found excuses to not finish his work, such as missing supplies or a broken pencil lead. Yes, summer school isn't that much different than the regular school year in that sense. I tried my best to motivate them with fun lessons and activities, yet there were two boys when Thursday arrived who hadn't finished all of their work.

When it was time to do our "dig," I explained that it was unfortunate they would not be participating that day because they weren't finished with their work. I told them they would need to work with my aide at the instructional table while the other boys participated. Both boys looked at one another, then back to me and shrugged as if to say, "Whatever."

The two boys were able to maintain their manner of disinterest as the activity got started at the back of the classroom with the boys seated on a shower curtain in front of an aluminum tray. Their indifference turned to interest when they heard the excited voices of the boys saying, "Look what I found! I think this is a fossil of a seashell!" Or another saying, "Jesse, I think I've found something but I don't know what it is. Can you tell?" Even though those two boys tried their best to look disinterested, they couldn't contain their questions when they heard the boys excitedly talking about what they were finding.

When the "dig" was completed and the students had gone to the bathroom to wash the remnants of sand off of their finds, each of the boys was able to share in front of the class what he had found. I offered the two boys the opportunity to be part of the class discussion and see what their classmates had located during the "dig." Even though they were slightly resentful of not being able to participate, they were still excited to be part of the conversation and see the artifacts.

One good outcome was that was the last time that any of the boys missed out on completing their weekly work from Monday through Wednesday. For the remaining three weeks, all six of the boys completed their work and were waiting with anticipation for Thursday to arrive.

On the last day of summer school, we learned we had about six aluminum trays left that hadn't been used. They still contained hidden treasures. I planned for the entire last day to be a "dig" with everyone having their own tray. They were beyond excited to know they would get to take everything they found in their trays home with them.

As the students began their digs, each one repeatedly called out to Jesse to help them identify what they had found. At one point, he turned to me and said, "Mrs. Adams, is it okay if I take my tray home if I don't have time today? I'm pretty busy here." Chuckling, I let Jesse know that would be fine.

End of the day takeaway

There are a few takeaways from this story. First, I'd like to address the issue of accountability. I have heard from teachers over the years that not allowing the boys to participate in the first dig because they hadn't completed the work was not fair and actually mean. To these educators I would like to respectfully disagree. While it was difficult to look at their disappointed and then sullen faces when they heard the news, the outcome was necessary if I wanted the students to understand the expectation to complete their classwork. Rather than viewing their inability to participate as a punishment, I think of it as a realization that they would be held accountable for the work.

It's often difficult to look into the eyes of educators who condemn me for these practices, and even more difficult to look at the disappointed eyes of my students; however, it is necessary if I want them to buy into the notion that work is expected and there are consequences for not meeting the expectations. This is an incredibly valuable life skill and the earlier learned the better. Everyone is held accountable for certain expectations as we mature, and our students will benefit from learning this standard while they are young. Furthermore, the boys did not repeat their behavior. They learned a valuable lesson that work is expected and rewarded with preferred activities, such as the "dinosaur dig."

In addition to the importance of accountability is the concept of teaching natural consequences to our students. Consequences, when applied, should be a natural outcome of the expectation that was not met. The students were very aware of what the outcome of failing to complete their work would be before making the decision to not work. When consequences are a natural product of the infraction, students learn to avoid the same consequence in the future. We lose the advantage of our students learning this valuable lesson when we assign consequences that do not match up with the expectation not met. For example, if I would have given the boys a consequence of missing recess for not completing their work, it might not have made the same lasting impression as losing out on a classroom project while they finished their work.

When we practice these consistent routines, students learn how to participate in a meaningful way in the classroom culture and they learn valuable life skills that will help them maintain jobs and other responsibilities in the future.

What can I say about Jesse? He learned that paleontologists study more than dinosaur bones, a fact I'm sure he hasn't forgotten. In addition, it's so important for every student to feel like he has an important contribution to bring to the class. Allowing students to shine in areas where they excel makes it easier for them to understand that they have talents and work harder at the tasks that are difficult for them. Imagine feeling as though you're just not good at anything. For many of my students, that's how they arrive. Through years of learned helplessness and failure, they've given up. It's sad to see students as young as 7-years-old who feel they have nothing valuable to bring to the classroom. Meeting each child where he is (academically and emotionally) and allowing them to feel that acceptance is a powerful way to establish a relationship with him.

Chapter 4:
Long Distance Runner
or Sprinter?

Change isn't easy for any of us.
However, when you start to see results through positive
changes in your students, you become energized and
empowered to try more and more strategies.
~Belinda Adams, Educator, Author

Teachers Need to Be "All In"

What do I mean by Teachers need to be 'All In'? Frankly, we need to be willing to keep trying, inventing, revising, and implementing new ideas until the last week of school. We also need to be ready to hang in there with those tough students who challenge us from the moment they walk in the door. If you think your students don't notice if you're a long distance runner or a sprinter when it comes to effort and tolerance, think again. Because they notice everything!

I've had students tell me, "You're gonna give up on me. Everyone else has." How sad. They push teachers, mentors, and sometimes, even peers away, keeping them at arm's length. A few of them really do want to be left alone. But the majority, I believe, want to see how hard we're willing to work to get past the rough exterior they've built up. They also establish these exterior façades to hide the fact that they don't want to get hurt again or be disappointed or let down again.

I've also had students who do something terribly wrong in the classroom, such as an angry outburst that breaks something or angry words that break school tolerance rules. Shortly afterwards, or in some cases immediately afterwards, they look at me to see if this means our relationship is over. Some have even asked,

"You're going to walk away, aren't you? What I've done or said is so ugly, you're going to give up, right?" Again, very, very sad.

As educators and role models, we've got to be able to show them we are capable of forgiving and forgetting. Yes, sometimes, reimbursement or a consequence is necessary; however, it's possible to do both while letting the student know you want to maintain your relationship. I tell my students that every day is a fresh start, a chance to try to do better at what we struggled with yesterday. And I can't just say it; I've got to mean it, and my actions have to prove it.

Lily: Alone

Lily was a 6th grade student who started school weeks after the rest of the class had begun the school year. I'm sure, walking in and realizing that these students had already developed relationships with one another, and feeling like an outsider, made Lily feel uneasy. She tried to mask those feelings behind a tough façade and an unfriendly tone for everything she said.

Many of my students had known one another for years and arriving in middle school as the youngest group of students in the school, they'd learned to stick together. I give them credit because when Lily arrived, they made efforts to include her in their reading groups or engage her in conversation about movies and music. She'd usually respond gruffly, giving them the impression she didn't care to share.

I'd seen many "Lilys" over the course of my teaching career. They arrived with armor so thick it made one wonder what could have happened in only 11 years of their young lives. I also recognized that Lily wasn't as disinterested in her classmates as she let on because I'd often see her watching them when they were goofing around or animatedly talking about their weekend plans.

When it came time to complete work, Lily tried hard to do as little as possible, often snorting or sighing as if the work she was asked to do was too challenging or too boring for her attention. However, unlike some of my students who had developed this habit for self-preservation to hide their deficits in grade level work, Lily was concealing the fact that she was very, very smart. In fact, when she did complete her work, I was surprised by her deep insights into the novel we were reading together and impressed with her writing ability.

One day, I called her over to the instructional table after the groups had returned to their desks and were working independently. She eyed me suspiciously but came to the table anyway. Quietly I said, "You are a very talented writer. I really like what you had to say about the character in the story." She exhaled loudly as if to let me know she wasn't impressed by my compliments and asked if she could return to her seat. "Sure," was all I could think to say, and she walked away.

I didn't let her standoffish behavior stop me from calling her up again to share my thoughts about her work; however, I did start adding small post-it notes on her papers with my thoughts about what she wrote. She usually read them thoughtfully before closing her notebook. One day, I wrote, "Wonder how he felt about being left out of the group?" I watched her face as she read the note, and observed how she grabbed her pencil and angrily scribbled over my words. Hmmm, maybe I was onto something.

Each week, I tried to find out more about Lily's background and experiences by writing similar notes for her. One note read, "I bet it's hard to be new in school, isn't it? Especially when everyone else seems to know each other." Rather than scribble on it or close her notebook, she picked up her pencil and wrote something. When class was over, I stepped to the door to release the students for their next class. When I returned to my desk, I saw my post-it with one word written in pencil in all caps, "YES."

I called Lily's home that evening to speak with her mother. I told her mother that I saw that Lily had moved quite a bit since starting 2nd grade. Lily's mother sighed and said, "That's when the divorce happened. We've been moving ever since it seems." I paused a moment to see if she was going to say more. When she didn't, I said, "Yes that can be difficult for everyone in the household. I'm wondering if you knew how smart Lily is?" When there was no response I continued, "Even with the moving, she's able to do grade level work, and she's an awesome writer." Lily's mother seemed floored, "You're kidding me! I mean, not that she's smart because I knew that, but just that you got her to do any work so you could *see* that."

That was the beginning of a home/school relationship that would bridge the gap for Lily and school. Her mother spoke to her that evening and told her that I called and what I had said. It seemed that Lily was touched by my phone call and obvious interest in her. Even though she didn't participate more or engage with her classmates, she no longer sighed or snorted and began to put effort into her classwork.

As we were getting ready for the holiday break, I asked the students how they would feel about a journaling project while we were off for two weeks. A few of them moaned, one or two nodded affirmatively, and Lily just sat there. The students became more excited about the idea when I explained that they could journal daily with words or drawings. Most of them decided to draw and I made sure everyone went home with colored pencils and their notebooks for the break.

I was pretty eager when we returned to school. I asked who had worked on the journaling project (because it had been optional) and was happy to see most of their hands go up. Lily didn't respond at all. I asked that everyone put their journals on my desk as they left and I'd be sure to look at them that evening.

My excitement over what the students had done came to a crashing halt when I opened Lily's journal. Rather than the detailed story I was expecting, I found she had scribbled on every page. Most of the scribbles were in pencil; however, a few of them were in red. I called Lily's mother right away to ask if everything was all right at home.

"She's not in trouble because the journaling activity was optional," I stated right away so her mother knew it wasn't about the lack of work or her grade. When I'd finished describing the pages, her mother was quiet for what seemed like an eternity. Finally, she said, "This is what Lily always does. She gets a teacher to notice her one way or another, and then she spoils it with something like this. It's not the first time." I chuckled a little and responded, "Well, she's never met a teacher like me. She's not going to scare me off this easily." Lily's mother seemed relieved and even more so when I asked her not to speak to Lily about my phone call.

I took special time on my post-its to Lily that night. I wrote a short note about a disappointment I'd had over break. I wrote another about something funny my dog had done. And on one or two pages, I simply put a post-it with a question mark.

The students were excited to read my comments and some chose to share a few of their journal entries with the class, especially those who had written about great Christmas presents or drawn funny illustrations. Lily sat quietly, deliberately letting me know she had no intention of sharing nor any interest in reading what I had written.

The next day, I found two post-its on my desk after she'd left class. She'd written briefly about a scary event over break when they were locked out of the house. And on another post-it (one where I'd written a question mark), she'd written the word, "Sad."

That was the last time that Lily scribbled in her notebook or crossed out my questions or comments. Instead, I'd find a post-it on my desk almost every day when she left whether I'd written her one or not. One day, she wrote, "I liked the shirt you had on today," with a smiley face. I responded by leaving her a post-it on her desk that read, "Thank you."

On one occasion, another of my female students had noticed that Lily sometimes had a post-it on her desk. She asked me, "What you always writing to that girl? She don't like any of us. Not sure what you'd say." I responded, "I don't think it's that she doesn't like any of us; I think she's just very shy because she's moved a lot and been to a lot of different schools." For most of my students, that was a topic they could surely understand. Many of them had changed schools and towns more than once and knew firsthand how hard it was to start fresh with new classes, new teachers, and new friends.

The following week, Lily was surprised to find two post-its on her desk; one from me and another from Anna, the girl who had asked me about her. Lily looked up questioningly at me when she saw the second post-it and I shrugged, smiled, and pointed towards Anna. Lily read the post-it and quickly wrote something on it. She looked towards me to see if I'd mind if she handed it to Anna, and I nodded my head yes. Whatever she wrote definitely made Anna smile, and a friendship started between the two girls. Before long, Lily was joining Anna's group for projects although she continued to stay quiet.

As spring break neared, I overheard Anna excitedly talking about her birthday party she'd have over spring break. I could see that Lily was listening intently to the conversation. Anna had asked before class if she could pass out her birthday party invitations at the end of class. We'd made a compromise that she could stand at the door and hand them out as students left so as not to make anyone feel left out. When she handed one to Lily on her way out, I could see that Lily was surprised and also happy for the invitation.

Lily made excellent academic growth that year in 6th grade. She found a group of girls to work with in class, and discovered a new friend in Anna. Unfortunately, as the year came to a close, Lily's mother informed me they would be moving over the summer. Sadly, I understood. I hoped Lily would remember the relationships she had built with Anna and me.

End of the day takeaway

For students of poverty, moving frequently is a common occurrence as housing instability is a traumatic fact of life for these kids. I'm always amazed at the resilience of some students who seem to make the moves with little emotional undertones and make friends easily. For most, unfortunately, that is not the case. Many, like Lily, struggle with new relationships and find it easier to stay to themselves while sending the message, "Stay away from me," with their demeanor.

In addition to the issue of transience was Lily's insistence on pushing me away. She'd made it clear through her responses that she didn't want to hear my compliments and wasn't interested in a conversation about her work. This is when I often feel that students are making sure their self-fulfilling prophecy doesn't fail. If they act and behave so no one will like them, they don't have to feel the sting of either being rejected by them or missing them when forced to move again.

It's important that we make every effort to make a connection with these students more than any. These are the students who are at risk for dropping out of school when they get old enough. Or worse yet, experiencing high anxiety, depression, or turning to self-medication to tune out the feelings of loneliness and isolation. Something as small as a post-it lightened Lily's load. It didn't take up a great deal of my time, and it let Lily know, "I see you. I'm not going away."

Even though she moved at the end of the school year, I like to think that Lily learned a valuable lesson about friendship. I hope she realized that she could have a relationship on her terms and at her comfort level. Regardless of whether or not it was a small post-it note or a long conversation, it was a connection.

Belinda Adams

Jacob: Been There, Done That

Jacob was a 5th grade student in my self-contained special education class. He made it clear from day one that he didn't belong in special ed, and he'd be out of my class as soon as he could. I responded, "Nothing would make me happier. I like when my students can join their friends in other classrooms."

Needless to say, I didn't explain to him that meeting grade level standards was the requirement for moving from my classroom to the general education setting because, quite frankly, I don't think he even realized he was behind his grade-level peers. Many of my students over the years had no idea that's why they were placed in my classroom. Some questioned me, and I answered honestly and always with the idea of hope that they could make enough progress to move on, but it all depended on their efforts.

Jacob was like many boys, and girls, I have had in class. He was athletic, quick with a comeback, attractive to his classmates, and wanting to work as little as possible. For many students of poverty, they just don't see the value of hard work in school because it isn't stressed as a priority at home. For them, school is more of something you "get through" so you can get home and enjoy your life. He liked basketball and running the neighborhood with his friends. Everything else in his life just seemed to get in the way of his favorite pastimes.

Jacob tried his best to do as little as possible. Unfortunately, with my high classroom expectations, this usually put us on opposing sides. He tested every limit in the classroom, from being out of his seat repeatedly to tearing up his classwork to walking out of class completely. Each time, I'd respond the same, "The work is not going away. You can do it now or do it later."

He definitely tested the "do it later" expectation because he frequently lost minutes at lunch recess or other preferred activities because he was expected to complete the work before enjoying those privileges. Sometimes, he'd acquiesce and do the work. Sometimes, he'd sit there staring at me sullenly. He seemed to be surprised, and then angered, when the same paper he'd left undone the previous day found its way to his desk the next day, even if it had been a paper he'd torn up or thrown in the trash. I always made extra copies so I was prepared.

One day, as he sat there stonily staring at the wall in front of him, I asked casually, "So what would it take for you to get your work done?" At first, he didn't answer and I wasn't sure if he'd even heard me. Then, he replied, "Nothing because I ain't doing it. "That's too bad," was my response, "because I know that the gym teacher was planning on going to recess with you guys on Friday. You might miss out because of your incomplete work."

Because everyone, especially the boys, liked the tall, athletic gym teacher, this was an attention-getter for Jacob. His head jerked up and I nodded. Right away, he got to work and finished in record time and headed off to lunch.

Jacob certainly didn't want to miss Friday's basketball-playing event with the gym teacher because he completed his work every day through Friday of that week. However, once the following Monday arrived, it seemed we were right back where we had started. More power struggles. More sullen looks. No work completion.

Thinking that basketball might be the ticket for motivating Jacob to work, I talked with the gym teacher. I asked him if he might be willing to shoot baskets with Jacob every Friday for 5-10 minutes if he was successful that week in completing most of his work. Fortunately, the gym teacher thought that was a great idea and said that Jacob would make a great basketball player someday if he kept working at it.

When I explained the incentive I had worked out with the gym teacher, Jacob shrugged and nodded because he didn't want to appear too eager or too grateful. After all, he was *still* going to have to do the classwork.

You might wonder if Jacob completed his work each week so he could play basketball? Nope, he did not. As with many students of poverty, they are prone to feeling the sting of upsets at home or periods of defiance, even if they lose out on a preferred activity. The first time I had to tell the gym teacher that Jacob wouldn't be joining him on that Friday, I felt very badly. The gym teacher looked upset that I was denying him the opportunity to shoot baskets with him. When I explained that I couldn't budge because it would throw all of our hard work out the window, he understood. He spoke with Jacob and said, "Jacob, sorry we can't shoot baskets this week. There's always next week. Let me know if I can help you get that work done because I'm gonna miss shooting baskets this week!"

Jacob earned Friday basketball time more Fridays that he didn't. I considered that a victory. In exchange, he completed his work and saw academic progress in reading and math. In fact, he showed more growth that year than the two previous school years combined. I hope that Jacob learned a valuable lesson: good work will be rewarded with things you enjoy.

End of the day takeaway

For Jacob, he always seemed to be testing and re-testing the boundaries and expectations that we had established for the classroom. I had to be strong, be consistent, and follow through with what I said each and every time. Any teetering on my part would have affirmed what he probably thought all along: if I hold out long enough, she's going to cave and give in.

In addition to consistent expectations and holding students accountable to meet those expectations, I also needed to find the right incentive that would motivate Jacob to complete this work. I'm very thankful the gym teacher also understood the value of offering a preferred incentive for a student who was difficult to motivate and was willing to give up a few minutes of his lunch time once a week to shoot baskets.

This story brings up another great point about motivating students of poverty. Studies have shown that the more positive relationships children can make with adults at school, the more it increases their likelihood of enjoying school more, working harder, and staying in school longer. Offering Jacob the opportunity to form a positive relationship with the gym teacher provided one more connection to school, strengthening that bond.

You see, it really does take a village to find the right balance for many of these students.

By working together, Jacob, the gym teacher and me, we were able to find an incentive plan that proved successful for Jacob. Not only did his mood and motivation improve, so did his academics! That's a win-win in my book.

Belinda Adams

Monica: Clothes Say Everything

When you work in a school with 99% free and reduced lunch where students come from tough neighborhoods with distrustful and unforgiving natures, you quickly learn to the read the nonverbal signals they are sending out. Asking a student who'd had a confrontation on the bus how their day was going in the hallway could result in a student who angrily said, "Mind your own, Mrs. Adams," rather than responding that it had been a bad day so far.

I discovered, after some fairly ugly one-sided conversations, that reading students' nonverbal cues and body language could save me a great deal of unnecessary confrontation. When students are posed as if ready for a fight, it probably isn't the best time to remind them to bring their notebook to class or ask if they'd remembered to bring in the book they had borrowed the week before. Nope, better to walk away and wait for another time to ask those questions.

One year, the 5th grade had a set of twin girls, Monica and Cherise. I had Monica in my classroom and Cherise was in the classroom across the hall. These two girls were well-known for their tough exteriors and most students, and staff, navigated clear of them in the hallways. As I observed them at the beginning of the year, I realized they rather enjoyed the mystique and terror their demeanors instilled in their peers and teachers alike. When students would step out of their way as they bulldozed down the hallway, it wasn't uncommon for them to sneak a sidewise look at one another and smirk.

Monica tried to push about every patience button of mine she could find. She blurted out, she got out of her seat repeatedly, and she smeared the notes on the whiteboard as she walked by to antagonize her peers who were finishing up their notes. When I finally felt my reserve of patience had been reached, I'd often put her in the hallway outside of my classroom near the door with her work and a whiteboard saying, "You're welcome to return when you're ready to follow the classroom expectations and show respect for your peers." To that, she'd smirk, and settle into the corner of the hallway where she proceeded to talk to every student who passed her and complete no work at all.

One morning, my partner teacher and I were standing in the hallway outside of our respective classroom doors as students began filing in. Under her breath, she whispered, "It's going to be a long day with those two – they're still wearing their pajama bottoms." As I followed her gaze, I saw Monica and Cherise pushing their way through the hallways, careless about who they shoved and sneering over their shoulders at anyone who dared to say anything to them. I looked at my partner teacher and rolled my eyes before mentally preparing myself for Monica to arrive in my classroom.

That afternoon after school, I was talking with my partner teacher, and told her she hadn't been wrong about the foul moods of Monica and Cherise when she saw them first thing in the morning. "When did you notice they have bad days when they're not dressed for school?" She looked at me quizzically for a few seconds, and then answered, "Not really sure when I really became aware, but today it hit me like a ton of bricks when I saw their faces and their pajama bottoms." She continued, "It seems like they often wake up later than they should to catch the bus, and their mother shoves them out the door whether they're dressed or not. We should take more notice and see if I'm correct in my hypothesis."

Once we started paying attention, there was a clear pattern to Monica and Cherise's moods. On days when they'd arrive at school wearing their pajama pants, and once even wearing their slippers, we discovered the girls were not in the best of moods and would do what they could that day to disrupt instruction and upset their peers in class. One morning, while I was attempting to speak with Monica in the hallway after having sent her out there for being disrespectful, I asked, "What happens on mornings when you and your sister almost miss the bus?" She debated answering my question at all, and finally said, "Our Mom works late three nights a week and we are supposed to get ourselves to bed. But we don't; usually we stay up playing video games or watching movies. That's how come we almost miss the bus because we're too tired to get up." Calmly I said, "You know, when that happens, you two work pretty hard to make everyone's life miserable." She looked at me, shrugged and said, "Well, that makes us all miserable then, doesn't it?"

There really wasn't much I could say to her after that comment. I felt badly that she was miserable, and even when made aware she was making others miserable as well, she didn't seem to care. I tried to look at her to see if I could catch a glimpse of realization or remorse in her eyes, but saw none. "It's unfortunate because you're a smart girl, and you might actually like school if you gave it a chance." To that, she merely turned away and sat down in the spot designated for her outside the classroom door.

Once my partner teacher and I became aware, there were other telltale signs that the girls had stayed up late the night before. It wasn't uncommon for the pajama pants to be accompanied by uncombed hair and missing backpacks. Those were the days we all wished we could just fast forward to dismissal because, when they arrived in that fashion, there was going to be little anyone could do to placate them.

When my partner teacher attempted to discuss the matter with their mother, she was shut down with comments such as, "I don't have any control over them girls when I'm not home" and "Sooner or later, they're gonna learn their lesson, I suppose." Even though my partner teacher attempted to explain that their late nights were negatively impacting their education, Monica and Cherise's mother refused to take any responsibility for their behavior and ended the conversation as quickly as she could.

Monica and Cherise headed off to seventh grade pretty much the same way they came into sixth; shoving their way down the hallways and showing little but contempt for their peers or teachers. I ran into a friend of mine who works at the high school several years later and asked how the girls were doing. She gave me a face that read, "It's best not to ask." I guess, Monica and Cherise were still going forward with what they had found worked for them; distancing themselves from their peers and teachers and completing as little work as possible. Sad, but true.

End of the day takeaway

The sad reality is that, even our most concerted efforts as educators, may not be enough to make positive changes for students of poverty. Many tell themselves they are comfortable right where they are, and they aren't interested in caring teachers who want to help them. And while most of us cannot imagine "comfortable" being a word that describes some students of poverty; however, we all acknowledge that change is difficult. Monica had spent the first 6 years of her academic life building up the emotional walls she brought with her to my class. And let's not forget that she had an ally in her sister, and she felt she didn't need anyone else.

When I first began working with students of poverty, I often misjudged the responses from parents like the ones provided by Monica and Cherise's mother. I took those statements of "I can't control what they do while I'm working" to be statements of disinterest. However, I discovered over the years of becoming more acquainted with my students' parents that this was more of a statement about her need to work to support the family. For many of us who come from middle-class families, our parents were home to help us with our homework each evening and make sure we got to bed on time. For many students of poverty, their parents must work the jobs that are available. Often, jobs that are accessible to parents with little education do not have working hours that are conducive for the parent to be home in the evening. In addition to evening hours, many of these jobs also have fluctuating hours that do not allow the parents the time or energy to be present for their children in the evenings.

I've had many parents over the years, for example, who worked the midnight shift. That meant, they needed to sleep during the day when their school-aged children were at school. However, what happens when the parent has another younger child at home? That doesn't allow the parent to sleep during the day. In these instances, parents must sleep in the evening so that the school-age children can watch after the younger children, not allowing them to offer assistance with homework or assure they have a predictable bedtime.

I've had to alter my train of thinking when it comes to parental attitudes about education in homes of poverty. Yes, I have had parents tell me that school never did anything for them, and they had no reason to be more encouraging for their child. In those instances, it's often a lose/lose situation for both the parent and the student. However, in most cases with my students and a lack of parent involvement, I've learned that there were often very good reasons for that lack of participation when I developed a relationship that encouraged the parent to share that information. Whether it was night hours that required they sleep in the evening or fluctuating, unpredictable hours that didn't allow for a routine, or a lack of transportation that caused them to lose a job, parents of poverty often have reasons for their lack of involvement in their child's education.

Part of the solution lies in our hands. We need to take the time to try to develop the relationships that allow parents to share with us candidly what is happening at home. I've had mothers say to me while crying, "I can't help her at home because I got to work. I have to be able to feed my babies." There's little as an educator and parent I can say to refute any parent's instinct to provide for her children. Our relationship comes into play when we demonstrate understanding and offer assistance.

If homework completion is an issue for a particular student and you know they won't have supervision at home to complete it, carve out 10-15 minutes at the end of the day so students can begin (or even complete) their homework. If it's getting to bed on time so they are ready to learn, work with parents and individual students to develop an incentive plan for preferred activities or treats that encourages them to get themselves to bed. Of course, the younger the student, the more difficult the latter can be. However, I've often thought, "Where there's a will, there's a way" and even my first-grade students could be taught what 8'o'clock looks like on an analog clock so they can go to bed.

It's all about problem solving and letting parents see your willingness to work with them, not judge them. In addition, it helps if your rapport with the student can build the bridge between parent/student/school connection.

Returning to Monica for a moment, I was shocked beyond words when she appeared at my classroom door after school during her sophomore year in high school. I recognized her immediately as Monica, but this was an entirely different young lady standing in front of me. She told me she was at school because she had been selected to lead a mentoring group of students from the 5th grade at our school. I guess, I must have looked shocked because she laughed and said, "Weird, huh?" I returned her smile and said I was glad to hear that she was finding herself and discovering her strengths. "I always knew you had the power to change your future," I said. She laughed again, "Well, not every day, anyway. I guess, I just needed to grow up Mrs. Adams." I smiled again and gave her a side hug as she left for her group.

The moral of this story is that we may never know if we made an impact on students in our classrooms. They appear to leave at the end of the year seemingly no better off than when they arrived. However, that should not keep us from trying, from reaching out, from making every effort to form a connection with our students. I am reminded that I must have made some form of impression on Monica if she wanted to drop by my room when she visited the school years later.

Chapter 5:
Nope, I Cannot Make
These Up!

Belinda Adams

Empowerment Often Equals Hilarity

There have been days when I've totally lost it. More times than I can count, I've placed my head down on my desk or instructional table. Often, during these times, I couldn't decide if I should laugh or cry. More than not, I'd generally start laughing because, after all, they are just kids and what do they say: "Kids will be kids."

This is especially true when teachers empower their students to have a voice. And if you're doing it correctly, you cannot give them a voice to share during instructional and discussions times without allowing them a voice at all times. I always told my students, "You can tell me anything as long as you talk respectfully." It takes a little while for students to completely buy into what I've said because it's a fairly new concept for them.

They might ask aloud, "So, if you mean anything, can I tell you this lesson seems stupid and I don't know why I have to do it and you won't get mad?" "Yep, that's what it means. You can share your opinion with me anytime. It doesn't mean I'm going to agree with you; I promise to hear you out."

One article explains the power of empowerment, calling it "...collective – the diverse imaginations, observations, opinions, hopes and dreams of students." The author continues saying, "By empowering students, you can engage them further in learning, provide a more democratic learning experience and, of course, find the most powerful resource in your classroom: us" (Svitak, 2012).

There's a caveat to instilling this powerful tool into your classroom: you've got to be ready for just about anything to come out of your students' mouths. Regardless of what it might be, it opens a door of communication that's often difficult to pry open when dealing with students of poverty. Their lack of trust in adults generally keeps them holding back, or waiting to speak until they're about ready to explode.

In my opinion, empowerment enhances the entire classroom environment. Others have commented on my classroom environment, by stating things like, "Your students seem so mindful of each other and you" or "How do you get them to work so hard if they're honest about how they feel about the work?" That's because I've empowered them to share and to feel as if they are a collective part of our classroom.

This gift of empowerment often leads to some pretty hilarious stories. I hope you enjoy them because I really cannot make these things up!

Watch Out for the Teacher

Jason was a student one year who made me laugh more than once a day. Usually, it was due to his outlandish comments that drove me to laughter because he didn't hold anything back, nor did he even try.

Even though he was several grades below academically, he seemed to compensate for that with his extraordinary perception and observation skills. It was these observations he'd share aloud that usually led me to laughter.

While teaching a lesson and being observed by the Principal for an evaluation, I was quite perturbed when Jason kept trying to interrupt. I'd already told the students I was being observed so they didn't spend the entire time saying, "someone's here" or "the principal's here," as if I couldn't see that for myself. So, it was frustrating when he persistently waved his hand in the air saying, "But Mrs. Adams…"

Finally, about 20 minutes into the lesson, I couldn't stand his interruptions for one more second. I snapped, "What is it Jason that just can't wait?" Nodding towards the principal and then towards the board, he stated, "Well, I thought on account of you getting watched and all that you might want to know you've got the wrong date on the board. Wouldn't want her to think you don't know how to read a calendar." As he finished, I felt my face go crimson as I turned to see that, indeed, the date was incorrect on the whiteboard. When I caught a glimpse of the Principal's face as she was attempting to hold in laughter, I started laughing aloud with her and thanked Jason for letting me know.

It was comments like those that came one after the other, day after day. It wasn't that he was trying to be disrespectful or make anyone feel incompetent, he just felt the need to share what he saw. I never admonished him for his observations, and told him more than once that he'd probably make a good attorney because no detail gets past him. He liked that idea.

The funniest moment occurred early in the spring. You see, we'd all been struggling with those February-March blues when the weather is crummy and the kids never go out for recess. The students were testy, often jumping at each other over minor things such as bumping into their desk or tripping over someone's shoe lining up. Unfortunately, teachers are prone to those blues, too. According to Jason and a few other brave students, I hadn't exactly been in the best of moods that week, and they, too were looking forward to some sunshine. I didn't realize the extent of my mood until Jason said what he said.

Jason's reading group was sitting with me at the instructional table, and I was struggling to get through the lesson with them. They were antsy, one didn't have a pencil, another had forgotten her book, and it seemed as if the lesson would go on forever. As I took a deep breath and drank from my coffee cup, Jason suddenly shoved his chair back from the table and yelled, "Everyone back up from the table. Mrs. Adams is out of coffee!"

First, shocked because he had shoved his chair from the table and yelled, then realizing that I had indeed finished my coffee led me to start smiling. When I saw his face smiling too, and the rest of the class trying hard not to smile, I burst out laughing. I laughed until I cried. Jason said, "It's okay, guys. I think she's losing it. But at least, she's laughing!" This only caused me to laugh even harder.

Jason had been right! I really was out of coffee, and probably soon out of patience as well. Moving back from the table probably wasn't a bad idea.

Belinda Adams

Jobs Can Be Dangerous

One year, I was struggling with how to get my students to take more responsibility for our classroom environment. They were hopelessly dropping candy wrappers on the floor and leaving them there, or throwing their school supplies half under their desk rather than placing them on the shelf below their chair, often providing me with something to trip over. Regardless of the chats we'd had about taking responsibility for our room, or the fact that I made them clean up before they could go to lunch; neither of which had made a dent in their behavior.

Then, "Eureka!" I had it! I'd devise some impressive names for classroom jobs, and rotate the jobs around the students each week. I thought I was brilliant. Instead of "Garbage Collector," that job was "Maintenance Operator. For those having issues logging onto their Chromebooks, we had "Computer Technician." For "Teacher Helper" we used "Teacher Assistant." There were a few other jobs as well.

It took a few weeks for the students to completely buy into the jobs; however, just like real jobs, every Friday was "payday." Our school used "Bucks" to reward students for demonstrating positive behavior, and they could use the "Bucks" to buy classroom supplies or small trinkets from the school store. The first time that Friday payday arrived, the students were sold on the idea.

"You mean, you're going to pay us for doing this stuff?" "Sure," I responded. "I get paid for the job I do and so should you. In fact, I'm giving 5 bonus bucks if you do a job above and beyond the expectation of the class. "Cool," was their collective response.

The jobs went very well for most of the school year. The students really enjoyed the responsibility, the rotation of the jobs, and the best part, getting paid. If a student was not living up to the expectation of their job, I'd say, "If you're not interested in your job and getting paid on Friday, I'm sure I can find someone to take over for you. I don't want to have to fire you." Knowing that another student would more than likely love to take over (because there weren't enough jobs for everyone to have a job every week) usually made the slacking student take his job more seriously. Even so, I had to be ready if a student said, "That's okay. I don't want to get paid." I would nod my head and rotate the job to the next person. It wasn't a big deal, and it was a choice each of them could make. Most of them, however, loved the idea of getting paid for a job well done.

One of the classroom jobs was to answer the classroom phone. You see, at the time, our classroom was very long in a rectangular shape. If I was at the other end of the room and the phone began ringing, it would usually stop ringing by the time I got to it. Humorous for some of the kids, for sure. Not so humorous if you're the student I'm leaving to go and answer the phone or the student seated next to the ringing phone. So, to solve the problem, I made one of the classroom jobs "Telephone Operator." That individual was in charge of answering the classroom phone if I wasn't in the near vicinity of it. We agreed on a two rules, which was the Telephone Operator wouldn't run for the phone unsafely or try to answer it if I was already there. (You see, that had happened once or twice already!)

One morning, while I was across the room working with a group of students, the phone began to ring. The Telephone Operator got up from her desk and walked towards the classroom phone, only to have it stop ringing when she was two steps away. She sighed, and went back to her seat. Within a minute, the phone was ringing again. She sighed again, walked over and answered the phone using the word choice we had agreed upon: "Mrs. Adams' room, how can I help you?"

I looked up as she answered the phone. I watched as she nodded her head, and muttered a few "Uh-huh's" and looked over towards me. After seeing me at the table, she said to the caller, "I know you'd like to talk with her right now but she's sitting down eating a donut and drinking her coffee. Can you call back?" and hung up.

I was mortified, because I had indeed been eating a donut and drinking my coffee, but I was also instructing a group at the time. I walked over to the phone and asked who had called. As she made her way back to her seat, she replied, "Oh, just the Principal. She said she'd call back."

Quickly, I dialed the Principal's office but never found out what she wanted because, when she answered, all I could hear was laughter. Still feeling a bit chagrinned, I hung up the phone and went back to teaching.

Note to self: when you encourage assertiveness, you've got to be ready for anything!

Paperwork Is Exhausting

In our district, Special Education Teachers are given an allowance of "Paperwork Days" so that we can have time out of the classroom to complete the additional paperwork required for special education students. I often try to minimize these days out of the classroom (not because I don't need them because I do) because the students generally did not respond well to having a substitute teacher.

Most classrooms struggle when their teacher is out, either due to illness or professional development. At our low-income school, however, substitute teachers had been known to leave in tears at the end of the day. With many of our students coming from tough neighborhoods, they could easily intimidate an inexperienced substitute or someone who is unfamiliar with their types of behavior.

Mine and my partner teacher's classes were no exception. Our classes were usually horrible when we were out. Students told lies, such as "she always lets us chew gum in class" or "she lets us leave 5 minutes before the bell to get to lunch on time." Students did not complete their work. The classroom was generally left in shambles. Worst of all, the particularly naughty students turned into pure demons when we were out of the classroom.

It didn't matter what we promised for good behavior. Or what we threatened for bad behavior. One year, our classrooms were nightmares if we were out of them. Our administrators were so overwhelmed with calls to the office when one or both of us were absent, they often begged us to alternate training days or to come in even if we were not feeling well.

This particular year, my partner teacher and I had two extremely, active and boisterous boys, Michael and Devin. I had started the year with both of them in my morning class and she had both of them in her afternoon class. We quickly learned that the two of them together was really too much to handle and get any instruction done at all. So, we had separated the boys, putting one in my morning class and one her morning class and switching our classes after lunch.

Even though singly they were still exhausting, they seemed more manageable when there was only one at a time. We were often reminded of why we separated the boys in the first place whenever they were together, such as during school assemblies.

Towards the end of spring when paperwork and report card deadlines get tight, my partner teacher and I decided we needed to take a paperwork day to assure everything got completed without needing to work until midnight each night. We picked a Wednesday, right in the middle of the week. Never a Monday because the students needed time to get back into the classroom routine. And never a Friday because students were beginning to unravel, thinking of the weekend ahead.

It seemed we had no sooner stationed ourselves in the corner of the media center with our computers barely opened that my substitute teacher called the librarian asking for me. She said the students were having a difficult time settling down and she couldn't get started with the lesson. So, down the hallway I stomped, wearing my most disappointed teacher face as I entered the classroom. After I'd sorted out the debate of which group was starting first at small group rotation that morning, I asked if there was anything else she needed before I left. She tilted her head towards Michael, my morning mischievous boy. I nodded. I walked over to Michael and asked what I could do to get him to start work. When he replied, "Nothing. I don't want to work," I responded, "That's your choice. All I'm asking is that you sit here quietly and let the rest of the class do their work." With that, I returned to the media center.

When the first call turned into the third call, and Michael being the reason for the second and third call, I made an executive decision. Realizing that I could spend the rest of the day running back and forth from the media center to my classroom, I told Michael, "Grab your supplies. You're coming with me." I took Michael back to the media center with me, placed his supplies on the floor, and pointed to the carpet next to my chair. "That's your spot for the rest of the day." Momentarily dumbfounded, Michael sat on the floor silently and looked up at me.

It was not even lunchtime before my partner teacher was called down to the classroom for her morning mischievous student, Devin. Even though her substitute teacher had held off longer calling her in the media center, it was apparent from the state of the substitute, and the classroom, that things hadn't been going smoothly. After she told my partner teacher about the things Devin had been doing, she decided she'd save herself a few more trips to the classroom, and told Devin to follow her to the media center.

When she arrived with him, she pointed to the carpet next to her chair and got back to work.

Because the two of us had grown accustomed to most of their shenanigans, they didn't distract us from doing our work all throughout the morning or while they ate their lunches together on the floor. Even though we were aware they were not completing any work at all, had started rolling around in their areas around our seats, and had attempted to construct about 10 paper airplanes, they were being quiet, and we were able to continue with our paperwork.

That was the year we had a brand new Assistant Principal who was well known for her short fuse. It seemed she had stopped in my classroom looking for me and found it "much louder than it should be." Consequently, she'd stepped over to my partner teacher's classroom and found hers to be "out of control." Both of these observations she shared with us as she marched into the media center to ask what we were doing. When we looked up from our computers, and simultaneously said, "Paperwork," she glared from the two of us to the two boys rolling around on the floor surrounded by paper airplanes and balls of paper. When both of us looked over our shoulders at the two boys and then back at her without expression, she turned on her heel and left the media center.

As the door closed behind her, Michael looked under the table at Devin and said, "Geez, you'd think she'd never seen us before." All my partner teacher and I could do was laugh quietly as we continued working.

"Isn't It Obvious?"

When you are a special education teacher and the Special Education Department Leader for your school, it's a given that peers and others will be stopping by with questions. It isn't easy to coordinate during planning periods when everyone's planning period was different, along with different lunch times. So, it was commonplace for teachers, the social worker, the psychologist, and administrators to stop by if something needed to be addressed or a question answered.

My class had become incredibly tolerant of these interruptions, and usually, would begin talking quietly to their neighbor while I quickly dealt with the situation or answered the question. Once the other adult had left the room, we'd pick up where we left off.

We had a brand new social worker that year, and she was new to the school system as well. "She's got a lot of questions," one of my students whispered under her breath when the social worker appeared in our classroom just about every day. After she'd left, I explained that it's difficult when you start a new job and it's good to have someone you can go to if you have questions. A quick nod of the head from my student was her only response.

One afternoon, while the students were working on a particularly engaging poster board project, they were excitedly calling me from one part of the room to the other so they could share the pictures they had located in the magazines I'd brought in. They were making collages of their personal character traits, something we had been covering in our social/emotional lessons. They were having a great time.

When the social worker came in with a question, they stopped calling my name until she left. Shortly after, a fellow teacher stopped in the room to ask about a student we shared. When I saw a few irritated looks coming her way from the students for interrupting our work, I asked if we could talk about it after school. A few short minutes later, the Principal arrived at our door. One of my more vocal students, Caitlyn looked up, sighed loudly and rolled her eyes. As the Principal walked towards me with a quizzical look on her face, she asked, "Caitlyn, what's going on with you today?" Without hesitation, she responded, "Ummm, it's obvious, isn't it?" When the Principal turned questioning eyes first to me then to Caitlyn, she continued, "Everyone keeps coming in here. Can't anybody do their jobs around here without Mrs. Adams? Can't you people see we are trying to get some work done here!"

Not being able to maintain a straight face any longer, my Principal quickly covered and said, "I heard about your project, and I just came down to take a look at them." "Well, it's about time someone realized we were working in this classroom," Caitlyn said.

Still smiling, my Principal walked around the classroom and let the students tell her about their projects. As she left, she whispered, "I'll ask you my question after school," and left chuckling.

Belinda Adams

Sketchy Connection

When you're working with students of poverty, they often struggle with emotional regulation and motivation amongst other things. Further, it's often difficult to encourage students to work when they don't want to work, see no value in the work, and have no consequences at home for not working. That's when it's time for teachers to get those creative juices flowing!

One year, I had a student who was so bright; he spent hours on his tablet at home and researched everything he was curious about. In fact, having a conversation with him was often like reading right from the Google search screen. However, where he excelled in his ability to discuss topics, he could not complete tasks required for his grade level such as formulating paragraphs or completing math calculations. Neither of these deficits seemed to matter to him at all.

Dillon was obsessed with RoBlox, a video game he often played, but more often, researched. He could tell you everything about the game from its creator to its recent upgrades and what features he could play without an actual subscription. However, whenever the discussion turned to actual classwork, he'd groan, slam his head onto his desk, and refuse to complete any work at all.

One day, while discussing the game with Dillon during snack time, he told me how excited he was to get home to his tablet that afternoon. I smiled, "Because you get to play RoBlox?" He responded, "No. I'll do that later. I'm excited because the new upgrade is coming soon with lots of new features. There's going to be news release about it today, and I can read all about what's coming!" "Well, that is exciting," I said as I returned to my desk. In reality, I was really thinking about how eccentric it was for an 8-year-old boy to be looking forward to reading a news release. Considering I hadn't gotten this boy to do much work for most of the year, I had a brainstorm.

The next morning I asked him about the latest news for his game, and he told me about it. I asked, "What do you think about writing a few sentences about that in your journal and sharing it with the class later?" "Sure," was all he had to say and got to work. Hmmm, I thought to myself; maybe I was onto something good!

Later in the day, I asked him how he would feel about earning minutes on my phone to read the news releases at school in exchange for completing his work. He thought for a moment, and responded, "Can I think about it?" Chuckling, I walked away.

The next day, he told me that my idea sounded okay to him. We agreed that he would earn 7 minutes on my iPhone for completing his morning work and he could earn another 7 minutes for completing his afternoon work. He thought that sounded fair.

After he'd complete his work, I would casually direct him to the brain break spot next to my desk and pull up the website on my phone. Dillon would sit quietly and read the news release, and occasionally, make a comment. Once he even asked for a post-it so he could write himself a note to look something up when he got home.

One afternoon while he was engaged in his afternoon incentive on my phone, he lifted his head and yelled across the room where I was working with a group of students. He shouted, "You've got an incoming call here … looks like SPAM … can I hit ignore?" I nodded my head yes, and he continued with his time. A similar event happened another day when he yelled, "Oh, Mr. Adams just texted you. Do you need to read it right now?" I shook my head "no" and he kept reading his news release. He soon became my social secretary, letting me know if I missed any calls or texts while he was researching. It was hilarious!

This strategy worked for Dillon for about 3 months. For whatever reason, he informed me one day, "I just cannot take it anymore. Either you need a new phone or your Wi-Fi service is just sketchy. I'll look it up at home."

Work over for Dillon.

Can You Come Back Later?

When you work daily with a partner teacher, sharing your group of special education students, it's fairly certain you'll become great friends. This was the case with my partner teacher. I taught reading and writing to her homeroom students and mine and she taught math, social studies and science to my students and her homeroom kids. We would switch our students each day after lunch. It was a great system because each of us got to teach subjects we were passionate about and we had to plan for less subjects. It was a win/win situation; both for us and our students.

Our students benefited because they were able to be instructed by two, very different personalities, and yet, two teachers who were willing to do whatever it took to help our students learn. We didn't let the fact that they were two or more academic years behind their same-age peers stop us from exposing them to rich, grade-level material, even though it had to be handed out in bite-sized bits. We didn't mind that most of our students came from low-income homes and were often very moody and indifferent. We saw both of these facts as a challenge to help them rise above their deficits and find and implement ways for them to be successful.

If you asked one of our students, I'm sure he/she would probably tell you, "They were pretty bossy! Never settled for anything until it was right." They might mutter something about being held accountable to complete the work, even if it meant we were all staying in from lunch recess to help them get it done.

They'd probably also tell you that my partner teacher and I laughed a lot, which is a great survival mechanism when you're working daily with at-risk students. You've got to be able to find the humor in situations. When one of us would forget something, the other would laugh, roll our eyes, and figure out how we were going to get by without the items. Or, as per usual, the copy machine died right in the middle of our copying, and we had to devise a creative plan on how to teach the lesson.

We especially liked to laugh at ourselves when we made a faux paus, which was pretty often. On one occasion, I got one of the charms on my bracelet caught in a hole in the keyboard of my computer and I couldn't get it out. After I'd had several of my students take a look and try to help, and still, I remained attached to my computer, I had one of the students open our adjoining door and ask my partner teacher if she could help me. When she saw me standing, helplessly holding my computer in one hand with the other wrist still stuck in the keyboard, she couldn't help but laugh so hard she was doubled over. When she finished laughing, she walked over, and said, "Maybe, it would help if you took off the bracelet first so we can take a look more closely." Well, duh, why hadn't I thought of that?

Because we had an adjoining door at the rear of our classrooms, we often propped it open. It allowed her students access to their desks if they'd forgotten anything or our students to easily step from one classroom to another if they were working on their homework and needed help with math, for example. Sometimes, if the students were working on a project, such as preparing posters for the fire department's fire prevention contest, my partner teacher and I would stand in the doorway, watching our students work and chit-chat.

Our students found us hilarious! One actually asked, "How do you guys find so much to talk about?" To this question, we laughed and said, "Oh, there's plenty."

One afternoon, shortly before dismissal for the day, we had the door propped open and we were talking quietly while the students had a few minutes to get started on their homework. They liked this opportunity because most of them could get their homework finished and leave it at school, having the rest of the night to themselves. My partner teacher and I were engaged in a fairly animated discussion, I guess, because I hadn't noticed that someone was standing outside of my door. I saw one of my students get up and walk over to the door and speak to the person on the other side. Then, he quietly closed the door and walked back to his seat.

When I went over and asked him who had been at the door, he answered very innocently, "It was the Principal. He wanted to talk to you, but I told him you and Mrs. P were talking again in the doorway, and he'd have to come back later." Both my partner teacher and I burst out into laughter! Out of the mouths of students, right?

Needless to say, the doors remained propped open, and our students benefited from our teamwork and spirit of collaboration.

End of the day takeaway

Probably the most powerful gift I can give my students is a voice. So many come into my classroom without the vocabulary to express themselves nor have they ever been encouraged to share what they know, think, or feel.

Voice is a powerful skill, and a life skill that becomes more valuable the more we use it! In an article about empowering students, author Svitak agrees that giving students a voice, along with other opportunities, emphasizes to your students that learning is a partnership. If you include the whole class as a group, learning is a collaborative effort. Svitak also encourages a few other strategies for empowering students in the classroom, including:

- ***Try to include students in making decisions*** *whenever we can. For example, in my classroom, this might look like allowing students to decide if they want to complete their seat work or their computer work first. For students who've never had the privilege of choice, it can be a powerful motivator. I also allow my students the choice of where to sit to complete their work. Some like to move away from others so not to be distracted. Others like to be in close proximity to me while working. The choice is theirs to make.*
- ***Work alongside your students.*** *An example in my classroom might be when I collaborate with a student about his idea for a story or project. They perceive that I'm working with them. Not only does this get students started with their work, it also reinforces the concept you are trying to teach.*

- ***Make technology use meaningful.*** *Rather than students putting their electronics away at class time, teachers can allow students to utilize their phones to access resource materials. In my classroom, when students ask about a topic, I often grab my phone and Google it, and we look at the information together. Or I'll use my phone to pull up images of a topic we are discussing. This gives me an opportunity to enhance what they are learning and provides the lesson with some authenticity.*

- ***Include real issues in your topics of instruction.*** *In classes with older students, this might include encouraging them to become involved in a real-life opportunity of what you are teaching, such as volunteering or becoming involved in a debate about opinions. With my students, I take the time to show them how what we are learning applies to real life. I might use a math problem to illustrate this is how a truck driver determines how many boxes he can transport in his truck. Or demonstrate how they can use the information in their day-to-day activities. One terrific example of this was when the occupational therapist and I did a lesson on recipes by allowing them to work together to create a treat. It was great timing because my students had been learning about fractions. By using fractions in our measuring of ingredients, students could see for themselves that fractions are a necessary skill for cooking, and life.*

(Svitak, 2012)

Empowerment is a compelling and positive part of your whole classroom climate. When others observe, empowerment looks like empathy and teamwork. For students individually, empowerment feels like choice and power, feelings that are often missed or discouraged at home. Teaching students of poverty to feel empowered is a gift that keeps giving. It's reciprocal and life-changing. Oh, and often funny too!

Wrapping It Up

I'm going to be transparent. Throughout this book, I've written about fellow teachers who have not shown empathy or understanding towards students of poverty. I've included myself in several of those stories to illustrate that none of us as educators are perfect. If anything, we learn from our mistakes and misfirings, and come out on the other side as better educators and better people, too. The first time I read Eric Jensen's book on poverty, I participated fully with our school's group book study. When that book study was done, I filed his book on the shelf and went back to business as usual. Which was not always pretty. I struggled with non-compliant, disrespectful students. I struggled because my students were not progressing academically.

It wasn't until I went searching for answers to solve my classroom problems that I discovered I had the power to change my classroom. As I've told teachers who dread each school day: "It's not like the buses will be coming from another part of town today. We're going to be getting the same students we had yesterday." We cannot wait for our students to change if we want to see results and maintain our sanity, and most importantly, continue to love our jobs. Change isn't easy for any of us. However, when you start to see results through positive changes in your students, you become energized and empowered to try more and more strategies.

In addition, I've tried to emphasize in many of my student's stories the need to team up with other teachers or support staff in your school to address the specific needs of these children. It really does take a village to make a positive impact on students of poverty.

Another example of forming that village approach is to understand the limitations of our students. For example, I've discussed repeatedly about the lack of trust these students have in adults. Once you've established that relationship and they've grown to rely on your consistency, just taking a day out of the classroom for professional development can seem like abandonment to them. Generally, they respond badly to this emotion. One approach my partner teacher and I established was that if she were going to be out of school for the day, for example, if a student chose to bring their supplies and work in my classroom all day, that would be acceptable. I set a desk at the back of the room for this purpose. That way, the student benefitted from the consistency of a familiar teacher, and the substitute in her classroom could teach the class without disruption. The same applied to my students when I was going to be out of the classroom. Not only are we addressing the students' need for consistency, once again, we are providing that student with a feeling of control and power over the situation. Rather than feeling they are a victim of a substitute that doesn't understand them, each student can make the decision to move to my classroom, or my partner teacher's, to work for the day.

Also, throughout this book, I hope you noticed the support, humor, and empowerment I was given by my administrators. That's an important element in developing a classroom management system and encouraging a warm classroom climate that cannot be ignored. That teacher/administrator relationship needs to be strong enough so that trust is established, and administrators feel confident that not only do you have your students' best interests in mind, you also demonstrate great academic and emotional growth at the end of the year.

I've had classes that were so unruly when I wasn't present that the music and gym teachers had threatened to make me attend class with them just so they would behave. When I'd hear about this, I'd often sit in on a music or gym class, working in the corner grading papers or lesson planning. While I was there, my students were respectful and followed the expectations of the music or gym class. You might wonder if I got involved with discipline or stared them down with stony eyes if they started to act up? I did not. I just sat there; however, my presence alone was enough for them to be respectful.

There are a few factors that resonate for me from these experiences. First, it's the safety issue. My students had learned to feel safe in my presence. With my predictable routines and nurturing ways, they'd found a place where they could let down their guard and worry less about saving face and participate more in class. The interesting fact here is that "safety" for these children isn't a place, such as my classroom; safety for them most often revolves around an individual or individuals and this feeling of safety goes with them. They feel safe in assemblies when I'm there; they feel safe during fire drills when I'm there; and they feel safe outside of our classroom when I'm there.

Secondly, it's the consistent expectations and consequences we establish for our classroom. My students know and respect that, in our classroom, we don't talk over one another. It's just rude. However, once out of our classroom, away from me, they seemed to forget that completely. Then, I realized, it wasn't about being out of our classroom. It was the fact that music and gym class didn't have the same expectations and consequences, and in some situations, there were none at all that they could count on. The lack of predictable expectations and consequences caused them to unravel at the seams. That's why so many schools have adopted Positive Behavior Intervention Systems (PBIS) that utilize universal language in all settings to provide the students with consistency, and hopefully, improve their behavior. The one caution with PBIS vocabulary and students of poverty is that much of the verbiage is geared towards a white, middle-class educational system that doesn't apply to them.

What do you say to a student, for example when you inform them that the way they had just spoken to their peer was not 'respecting all others,' and the student looks at you and says, "I don't care." Because in their mind, that might very well be true. Maybe they don't care that the way that they spoke disrespected the person they said it to. However, if one of the classroom expectations is that we respect each other so that everyone has a chance to be heard, students embrace the idea that expectations are beneficial to them and are more apt to follow them. Another example is telling students that they are not 'respecting the learning of others.' Once again, many of my students would answer, "Who cares?" They might be sharing very honestly their true feelings. However, when we restate the expectation explaining that "it's hard for me to expect others to be quiet while you're working if you're not willing to do the same for them." In many ways, we've got to approach the issue of following expectations as a bill of rights for the students. When they feel they are gaining something by following the expectations, it's been my experience that they're more willing to follow them.

Lastly, there's something I say quite frequently that I'm sure many teachers have grown to dislike and that is, "They are children. They are learning how to do what's right and fix what's wrong. We cannot expect perfection or we're going to be disappointed every time."

In conclusion, I want to remind you that poverty is very real to the children who live it every day! I've never experienced poverty so I don't know what it feels like to go without dinner or clean clothes or school supplies. I can only begin to imagine how powerless it makes these young children feel to experience poverty as an everyday living situation. As educators, we have the power to negate some of its effects and help students overcome the deficits poverty may bring to their education. It is possible. With an open mind and a heart ready to give and forgive, we can show these students that school is a place they want to be. The stories of my students should provide hope for our future students.

Belinda Adams

The Realities of Generational Poverty

If you're interested in learning more about how generational poverty impacts education, there are several great books out there. Because it's important to be aware of the types of poverty you are dealing with in your classroom. "Situational poverty" is poverty which occurs as a result of a life-changing event, such as a divorce or loss of job and/or home. Conversely, "generational poverty" is defined as having lived in poverty for at least two generations, especially if the family lives with others who are from generational poverty (Payne, pg. 61). For many of my students, who lived in a low-income housing project near my school, generational poverty was the circumstance.

If you've never heard a student describe, in detail, being evicted from his home by the police, or the inability to stay clean when she's living in her car with her mother and siblings, or the impossibility of doing homework when the electric company has shut off his power, you have never come face to face with a student of poverty who trusts you. Because that trust is instrumental if they're going to share those heart-wrenching, painful realities with you. Yet, knowing those realities (or understanding these disparities might be part of a student's life) might be the only way you can help this child overcome the sadness and hopelessness that poverty brings.

Some of the characteristics of generational poverty comprise:

- Instability in housing, including periodic homelessness
- Food insecurity
- Unemployment/underemployment
- Crowded housing/lack of personal space
- Uneducated/undereducated adults
- Limited knowledge bases
- Exposure to violence, addiction, and incarceration
- Unaddressed physical and emotional issues (Payne, pg. 62).

Not only did my students face the traumas of poverty, as listed above, many of them didn't know anything else. With resentment, they accepted that this was their lot in life, and few had any hopes for a better future or even how to take steps to improve their situation in the future. A few tragic short stories to illustrate my point:

Gretchen was a girl in my 6th grade class. She was very precocious, and didn't hesitate to speak her mind or share her sharp attention to detail. I'm not even sure how the conversation began. However, one day towards the end of school, Gretchen asked me how much money I got on my LINC card each month. When I answered that I didn't have a LINC card, she stared at me incredulously. Quietly, I said, "Not everyone gets a LINC card." Her response was instantaneous, "Sure, they do, Mrs. Adams! Come on, just tell me. How much you get on your card?" Once again, I told her that I didn't get a LINC card and that's why I had a job so that I could buy the things my family needs. After nearly

10 minutes of conversation, I was no closer to convincing Gretchen that I did not have a LINC card. As the bell rang to signal the end of the day, Gretchen yelled over her shoulder, "Fine, Mrs. Adams, don't tell me. I mean, if you didn't want to tell me how much you get, you should've just said so," as she walked out the door. You see, it wasn't that Gretchen was being disrespectful towards me; it was that she didn't know any different than her own reality and the reality of the families that she knew.

Roberto was a boy in my 5th grade class. One day, he was complaining (again) about the work he was being asked to do. Finally, he yelled, "Oh, what's the point of all this?" When I asked what he was talking about. He responded that he just didn't see the point of doing all this work in class. I told him that the work we did in class would help him gain skills and those skills would help him get a job and be successful. He looked at me with a great deal of skepticism. Later, when he came to reading group, I asked him to stay behind so I could talk to him for a minute. "You trust me, don't you Roberto?" He agreed with a bob of his head. "Then you have to believe me when I tell you that what we do here in class matters. I am teaching you the skills you need to do the things you want to do, like get your driver's license and a job someday." Still, he seemed unconvinced. When I asked what part of the work he found so pointless, Roberto said, "All of it. I just don't see how any of this is gonna help me. I'm still gonna live where I live and nothing is gonna change." I thought for a moment before I answered, "Sometimes, it feels that way. I get it. But, I really believe that if you work hard at something, such as learning in school, you are going to have benefits later." For many students, like Roberto, the way that they see things is often the way they think it will always be. It takes a great deal of convincing and

165

proving daily that they do have the power to make positive changes for their future.

Mandy was a girl in my 6th grade class. She struggled greatly in class because she was working at a 4th grade level. Some of this delay was due to her lower cognitive level; however, I had come to realize that a great deal of her deficits were due to her belief that she couldn't do any better. Even when she would experience success at a task, it was difficult for her to celebrate because, when complimented or congratulated on her efforts, she'd respond, "Well, I'll probably forget it tomorrow." About mid-year, I called Mandy's mother to share my concerns about her low motivation to gain academic skills. I was shocked to silence when the parent's response was, "All my kids are slow. I was in special ed when I was in school. She's just gonna be slow like the rest of them." This attitude illustrates the magnitude of beliefs in families living in generational poverty. Mandy didn't think she could do any better because her mother didn't think she could do any better. And because she lacked motivation and positivity, she was living out her own self-fulfilling prophecy of failing at school.

These are just a few of the stories of students I've had in my classroom. I have many more. However, I'm sure you can see the hopelessness and skewed thinking that occurs in homes where generational poverty is a reality. It takes a great deal of perseverance and downright stubbornness to roll up your sleeves as an educator and say, "Nope, not on my watch!" I've always felt determined to do what I can to enlighten my students, give them a glimpse of what could be, instill them with a sense of hope, and work diligently to provide them with instruction that builds skills they can use to make change happen, now and in the future.

Can You See Me Yet?

Reflection of Book Concepts & Implementation Guide

Reflection & Implementation

If you've been an educator for more than three years, you'll probably agree that professional development is difficult for a number of reasons. First, these workshops and trainings usually occur during the school year. We must create detailed lesson plans for our substitute teacher and pray that our students behave appropriately and get *some* work done while we are out. Second, as we sit there during our training, we are besieged by thoughts of things we must do. Almost unconsciously, we began making lists and our thoughts wander away from the topic of the workshop. Finally, even when I have experienced an excellent workshop which generates great thought-provoking ideas as I sit there, too often I return to my classroom and file the handouts in my professional development folder and tell myself, "I'll get to those great ideas when I have a free moment." Unfortunately, if you're like me, there rarely seems to be a free moment, and those great ideas begin to gather dust in that folder and are soon forgotten completely.

I hope you enjoyed reading my book. I also hope, at some point throughout, you've thought, "Yes, I had a student like her!" or "That's a great idea! I could use that at the beginning of the year." The following reflection and implementation guide will provide you with a great place to write down and organize those thoughts. With any luck, you'll see ways you can develop and incorporate my strategies, and some of your own, into your classroom right away.

Please grab a pen and a cup of coffee, and make some notes. I'd love to hear from you regarding your reflections and plans for implementation. Further, after you've tried a few strategies, I'd love to hear about their success or need for tweaking. Let's get started!

What is your knowledge or experience in working with students from low income families?

_____

_____

_____

What specific characteristics did you see in your students? Or if this is your first exposure to low income students, were there common student characteristics you noticed while reading my students' stories?

_____

_____

_____

What specific challenges did you experience while working with these students? Or if this is your first exposure to low income students, did you take note of any specific challenges that were common in my students' stories?

_____

_____

_____

In thinking about the chapter <u>Are You the Fuse? Or the Diffuser?</u>, did you feel that you fell into one of those two categories more times than not? (Remember I mentioned that it is possible for us to be both; it's a question of which one are you predominantly?)

_____

_____

What are some of the common themes you recognize when you are serving as the fuse in your teacher/student relationship(s)?

_____

_____

_____

Throughout this section, my strategies rely heavily on developing connections and rapport with students to avoid being the fuse in the relationship. What strategies have you used when you have felt you were part of what was setting off your student(s)?

_____

_____

_____

_____

_____

After reading the stories of these students, were you able to identify any specific strategies you might like to try to assist you in building relationships?

_____

_____

_____

_____

After reading the stories of these students, was there one particular story that resonated with you? What about the story struck a chord? How can you use this connection with the story to help you implement relationship-building strategies in your classroom?

_____

_____

_____

In the section, <u>Teacher: Friend or Foe?</u>, can you identify with times you may have been viewed by your students as a foe, or someone they cannot trust or allow into their inner circle? What were some of the characteristics of that relationship?

_____

_____

_____

Can you recall students who considered you to be their friend, an ally in the learning process? What were the characteristics of those relationships?

_____

_____

_____

Have you had students like Markise and Jaylen who struggled to have a voice to express their wants and needs? How has their lack of voice impacted the classroom?

_____

_____

_____

After reading these children's stories, were you able to see strategies you might implement in the future that would benefit students who need assistance in finding their voice? What might you try?

_____

_____

_____

In reading about Dan Siegel's 4 S's of Attachment (Safe, Seen, Soothed and Secure), can you see how these positive elements are necessary if students of poverty are going to relax and engage in learning? If so, what areas do you feel you could improve upon to accomplish the 4 S's in your classroom?

_____

_____

_____

_____

Don't forget your strengths as well. In what areas do you already excel in building attachment? How can you capitalize on those successful strategies for even greater success?

_____

_____

_____

What were your thoughts on the chapter <u>Teacher or Lecturer</u>? Can you see times during your teaching experience when you have filled these roles? What did the role of the lecturer look like? What were the responses of your students?

_____

_____

_____

What did the role of the teacher look like? What were the responses of your students?

_____

_____

_____

Can you see opportunities in your current lesson planning when you can allow your students to become more engaged in guiding their instruction? What does that look like? Where might you begin to implement this strategy?

_____

_____

_____

What drawbacks do you envision when releasing some of the teacher controls on student instruction? What expectations could you put into place that would diminish the drawbacks?

_____

_____

_____

In the chapter, <u>Long Distance Runner or Sprinter</u>, can you picture times when you have played these roles in your approach to a student? What was the outcome of that approach?

_____

_____

_____

What can be the negative impact when students believe you are a "sprinter" and that you will give up on them eventually? In your experience, have their attitudes been detrimental to their learning and the overall climate in your classroom?

_____

_____

How might you address students who challenge you about giving up on them? What strategies might you employ?

_____

_____

_____

What do you think are the characteristics of a "long distance runner" teacher? What are some of the key traits you must internalize and display?

_____

_____

Just for fun, can you recall your funniest classroom experience? Jot down a few notes. You might surprise yourself with what you think of when you start remembering.

_____

_____

_____

_____

_____

_____

The funny stories in this book revolve a great deal around the concept of empowerment and instilling in my students the knowledge that they have a voice in my classroom at all times.

Even in these humorous stories, there is often a gem of a classroom management strategy that shines through. Can you see a common theme in your stories? If so, what is it? How might you continue to foster it?

_____

_____

_____

As with most new ideas, there seems to be little time (and energy) to implement them into our classroom. When thinking about where to begin to incorporate some of these ideas, two fairly easy places to start might be to (1) assign jobs to your students, thus providing them with a sense of control and power in the classroom, and (2) identify ways you can provide your students with a voice or choice for the methods they use to complete work (such as typing, writing or drawing). If you were to select two strategies from this book, or your own as you were reflecting, what would they be?

1. _____

2. _____

How might you incorporate them into your classroom next week? Or next semester? Or even next school year?

_____

_____

_____

What is one overriding thought or strategy you'd like to keep with you each day as you look into the faces of your students? How might this thought or strategy benefit your instruction and your students?

_____

_____

Again, I encourage you to share your comments, your reflections and your ideas with me! I meant what I wrote that I am always learning. What better teachers than fellow teachers? You can also visit my Facebook page or follow me on Amazon. Can't wait to hear from you!

Teachers REACH for Success on Facebook or Anchor Book Press, 440 W Colfax St, Unit 1132, Palatine, IL 60078

Bibliography

American Psychological Association. Effects of Poverty, Hunger and Homelessness on Children and Youth. 2009. https://www.apa.org/pi/families/poverty

Dobrin, Arthur, D.S.W. The Effects of Poverty on the Brain: The brains of poor children are atrophied but can rebound. Psychology Today, October 12, 2012. https://www.psychologytoday.com/us/blog/am-i-right/201210/the-effects-poverty-the-brain

Fay, Jim & Funk, David. *Teaching with Love and Logic*. The Love and Logic Institute, Golden, CO, 2007.

Ingram, EdD, LCSW, Brenda. Trauma Informed Approach to Classroom Management. https://achieve.lausd.net.

Jensen, Eric. *Engaging Students with Poverty in Mind*. ASCD, Alexandria, VA, 2013.

Michie, Gregory. *Holler If You Hear Me*. Teacher's College, Columbia University, New York, NY, 2009.

Payne, Ruby K., Ph.D., *A Framework for Understanding Poverty: A Cognitive Approach*. aha! Process, Inc., Highlands, TX, 2013.

Pierson, Ruby. Every Kid Needs a Champion. https://www.ted.com/talks/rita_pierson_every_kid_needs_a_champion/transcript

Raver, C. Cybele, Blair, Clancy, Garrett-Peters, Patricia and Family Life Project Key Investigators. *Poverty, household chaos, and interparental aggression predict children's ability to recognize and modulate negative emotions. National Center for Biotechnology Information, U.S. National Library of Medicine, 8600 Rockville Pike, Bethesda, MD 20894 USA.* https://www.ncbi.nlm.nih.gov/pmc/articles/PMC4682352/

Rocheleau, Jackie. How Poverty Shapes a Child's Mind and Brain. BrainFacts/SfN, October 14, 2019. https://www.brainfacts.org/neuroscience-in-society/law-economics-and-ethics/2019/how-poverty-shapes-a-childs-mind-and-brain-101419

Siegel, MD., Dan and Bryson, PhD., Tina Payne. What is A Whole-Brain Child? The 4 S's To Ensure a Secure Attachment. January 15, 2020. mindbodygreen.com/articles/how-to-ensure-your-child-has-a-secure-attachment.

Svitak, Adora. 5 Ways to Empower Students: Giving them a voice in their own education. Edutopia, February 8, 2012. https://www.edutopia.org/blog/empower-students-adora-svitak

About the Author

Belinda Adams is an elementary teacher. She has degrees in psychology and special education. She has taught students in kindergarten through eighth grade. She has taught general education students, students in special education, and students in regular education who needed remediation. With success rates that exceed expected yearly growth, Belinda is always available to discuss solutions for those dealing with difficult students because she believes every student *wants* to learn when provided the *right* motivation and support.

Certified as a Childhood Trauma Professional, Belinda devotes hours each year reading new studies and books about trauma, poverty, and helping children find success in the classroom. She has presented to her peers on the topic of accommodating special needs and at-risk students in classrooms. She continues to build her knowledge base by attending conferences and seminars, and she is always interested to learn from her peers about best practices that bring results.

Before becoming a teacher, Belinda worked in the business world and wrote a weekly editorial for a northwestern Illinois newspaper. In her spare time, oh wait, Belinda is a teacher and an author, she doesn't have spare time. She lives in the Midwest with her husband, her son, and her dogs, Murphy & Suzy Q.

Other Books by the Author

Belinda's Award Winning and Top Selling Book:

Can You See Me?

 Using Understanding to Help Students of Poverty Feel Seen, Heard & Valued in the Classroom

Don't Look Too Closely:

 What Children of Trauma are Hiding and How You Can Be the Difference for Them

e-Learning: It's Not for the Faint-Hearted

 (A light look at remote learning through a teacher's eyes.)

If Only She Knew:

 Engaging the Whole Student with Trauma in Mind

Mom's Gift:

 No Problem Is Too Big for Mom & Me

     (Children's Picture Book)

Parents REACH for Success:

 4 Strategies to Give Your Child the Growth Mindset for School Success

REACH for Success:

 4 Strategies to Positively Impact Your Classroom

There's More to Me Than She Can See:

 Engaging the Whole Student with Trauma in Mind

Why Math? Mental Anguish to Humanity:

 Engaging At-Risk Students in Math and Science When the Teacher Hates Teaching It

Future Books by Belinda Adams

Throw Away Kids

When most see those three words, it is the low-income and foster care situations that probably come to mind first. That is NOT what this book is about. Special education colleagues and diligent advocates for students with special needs, Carol Pirog and Belinda Adams, collaborate as they jump onto the slippery slope of issues plaguing students labeled as needing "special education".

Breaking protocols of what might be considered politically correct, Carol and Belinda shed light on who these *Throw Away Kids* are and our obligation, as educators and parents, to turn the tide in their favor. *Throw Away Kids* are kids of every ethnicity and income range. They are the kids that need advocates to help them find their own voices and empower them as they move toward success.

I'm Different & That's Okay with Me

The second children's picture book from Belinda features the perspective of her 8-year-old son, Austin, as he learns to accept and overcome the challenges of his learning disability. With thoughts and feelings that will bring tears to your eyes, along with the honest, genuine voice of a young boy who will bring laughter to your lips, Belinda shares his journey to find his way. This book is a must have for parents, educators, social workers and all those adults who work with children who struggle with accepting their own differences and learning to be successful despite them!

Made in the USA
Monee, IL
01 November 2020